CAMPAIGN 351

VELIKIYE LUKI 1942–43

The Doomed Fortress

ROBERT A. FORCZYK   ILLUSTRATED BY PETER DENNIS

Series editor Marcus Cowper

OSPREY PUBLISHING
Bloomsbury Publishing Plc
PO Box 883, Oxford, OX1 9PL, UK
1385 Broadway, 5th Floor, New York, NY 10018, USA
E-mail: info@ospreypublishing.com
www.ospreypublishing.com

OSPREY is a trademark of Osprey Publishing Ltd

First published in Great Britain in 2020

A catalogue record for this book is available from the British Library.

ISBN: PB 9781472830692; eBook 9781472830708; ePDF 9781472830715;
XML 9781472830722

20 21 22 23 24 ▪ 10 9 8 7 6 5 4 3 2 1

Maps by www.bounford.com
3D BEVs by Paul Kime
Index by Zoe Ross
Typeset by PDQ Digital Media Solutions, Bungay, UK
Printed and bound in India by Replika Press Private Ltd.

Artist's note

Readers may care to note that the original paintings from which the colour plates in this book were prepared are available for private sale. All reproduction copyright whatsoever is retained by the publishers. All enquiries should be addressed to:

Peter Dennis, Fieldhead, The Park, Mansfield, Notts, NG18 2AT, UK
Email: magiehollingworth@yahoo.co.uk

The publishers regret that they can enter into no correspondence upon this matter.

Osprey Publishing supports the Woodland Trust, the UK's leading woodland conservation charity.

To find out more about our authors and books visit **www.ospreypublishing.com**. Here you will find extracts, author interviews, details of forthcoming events and the option to sign up for our newsletter.

Author's acknowledgements

I wish to thank Nik Cornish for his help with this project.

Dedication

In remembrance of MSG Michael B. Riley, 2nd Battalion, 10th SFG (A), KIA, enemy small-arms fire, Uruzgan Province, Afghanistan, 25 June 2019.

Glossary and abbreviations

Aviatsionnyi Shturmovoy Korpus (ShaK)	Assault Aviation Corps
Bombardirovochnaya Aviatsionnyi Divisiya	Bomber Aviation Division
Bombardirovochnaya Aviatsionnyi Korpus	Bomber Aviation Corps
Feld Ersatz-Bataillon (FEB)	field replacement battalion
Gvardeiskyi Isrebitelnyi Aviatsionnyi Polk (GIAP)	Guards Fighter Aviation Regiment
OKH	Oberkommando des Heeres
HKL	Hauptkampflinie – main line of resistance
Isrebitelnyi Aviatsionnyi Divisiya (IAD)	Fighter Aviation Division
Isrebitelnyi Aviatsionnyi Korpus (IAK)	Fighter Aviation Corps
Isrebitelnyi Aviatsionnyi Polk (IAP)	Fighter Aviation Regiment
Kradschützen	motorcycle infantry
MRL	multiple rocket-launcher
NKVD	Narodny komissariat vnutrennikh del (People's Commissariat for Internal Affairs)
RVGK	Rezerv Verkhovnogo Glavnokomandovaniya – Stavka Reserve
Schützenpanzerwagen (SPW)	armoured infantry vehicle
Vozdushnaya armiya (VA)	Air Army
Voyenno-Vozdushnye Sily (VVS)	Soviet Air Force

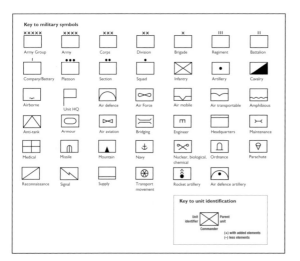

Key to military symbols

Key to unit identification

PREVIOUS PAGE
German tanks lie knocked out in the ruins of Velikiye Luki.
(Author's collection)

CONTENTS

ORIGINS OF THE CAMPAIGN

During the early days of the Novgorod Republic in the 12th century, the Russians built a number of fortified towns to protect their border regions against foreign invasion. One of these towns, Velikiye Luki, located 245km south of Novgorod, started out as a wooden-walled settlement on the banks of the Lovat River. Gradually, the fortifications were improved and a Kremlin was built on the western side of the river, but the Poles destroyed the fortress of Velikiye Luki in 1580. Eventually, the Russians rebuilt the fortress, but it was destroyed by fire. Due to the threat of Swedish invasion, Peter the Great ordered the construction of a modern bastion-type fortress in Velikiye Luki, armed with artillery, which was completed in 1708. However, after the defeat of the Swedes, the fortress in Velikiye Luki no longer served a valid military purpose and played no role in Tsarist Russia's later wars. By the early 20th century, the city gained some importance as a transportation node, once rail lines were built; the train station in Velikiye Luki became a transfer point between the standard-gauge rail track used in Western Europe and the broad-gauge rail tracks used in most of the USSR. Given the limited transportation infrastructure in northern Russia, Velikiye Luki was noteworthy as one of the few hubs in an otherwise remote region. By the start of World War II, Velikiye Luki had a population of about 35,000.

When the Oberkommando des Heeres (OKH) planned Operation *Barbarossa* in 1940–41, its staff did not anticipate positional warfare in the remote marshes and forests of northern Russia. Rather, Heeresgruppe Nord (Army Group North) was expected to rapidly push through the Baltic States and reach Leningrad in about eight weeks. Heeresgruppe Mitte (Army Group Centre) was supposed to destroy the Soviet formations along the Minsk–Smolensk axis, then capture Moscow once Soviet resistance in the centre of the front had collapsed. Since the Germans lacked the troops to maintain a continuous front, Heeresgruppe Nord and Heeresgruppe Mitte would only maintain tenuous contact during their advance, but the OKH assessed this as a reasonable risk in a presumably short campaign. Any remaining Soviet forces in the area between Leningrad and Moscow would be dealt with in subsequent mop-up operations – that was the plan.

However, Operation *Barbarossa* did not go according to plan. Heeresgruppe Nord romped through the Baltic States with ease but was delayed on the Luga River for a month by intense Soviet resistance. Meanwhile, Heeresgruppe Mitte pushed on to Smolensk but was struck by repeated Soviet counter-attacks, which brought its advance to a virtual halt for three weeks. During the Battle of Smolensk, the OKH first began to notice that the gap between Heeresgruppe Nord and Heeresgruppe Mitte might be exploited by the Soviets and directed additional forces to cover this perceived vulnerability. Stavka (the Soviet High Command) had raised the 22nd Army, with its headquarters in Velikiye Luki, and ordered its commander, General-leytenant Filipp A. Ershakov, to hold the Polotsk Fortified Area north of Vitebsk. Hitler and the OKH became nervous that the Soviet 22nd Army could use the fortified area as a springboard to launch a counter-attack into the flank of Heeresgruppe Mitte. In fact, Stavka was considering this course of action and had already sent armour to reinforce Ershakov's 22nd Army. However, the Germans struck first. The 3.Panzer-Armee detached its LVII.Armee-Korps (mot.) to secure the area north of Vitebsk with just two divisions – 19.Panzer-Division and 18.Infanterie-Division (mot.). Amazingly, LVII.Armee-Korps (mot.) was able to overrun part of the Polotsk fortified area and encircle most of Ershakov's 22nd Army, then push on to seize the town of Nevel on 15 July 1941. Two days later, a *Kampfgruppe* from 19.Panzer-Division occupied the rail junction at Velikiye Luki.

Enraged by the sudden loss of Velikiye Luki, which was also a major supply depot for the Red Army, Stavka ordered the remnants of the 22nd Army to launch an immediate counter-offensive. Reinforced by the fresh 48th Tank Division, Ershakov struck the LVII.Armee-Korps' tenuous lines of communication. The Germans were badly outnumbered and strung out across a wide swath of marshy, wooded terrain, which made them vulnerable to encirclement. After several days of fighting, the Germans evacuated Velikiye Luki and pulled back to Nevel, enabling the Soviet 22nd Army to march in – the first Russian city liberated in World War II. However, once the Battle of Smolensk was concluded and the remnants of the Soviet Western Front were in retreat, Heeresgruppe Mitte diverted six divisions to clear up the situation around Velikiye Luki. In mid-August 1941, the Germans struck, and after a week of heavy fighting encircled Velikiye Luki and then crushed the pocket, taking over 24,000 prisoners. The Germans reoccupied Velikiye Luki on 26 August and thereafter the Germans pushed on to Toropets, then towards Ostashkov, but were eventually stopped by the resistance of the Soviet North-Western Front. Meanwhile, the Germans enforced a brutal occupation in Velikiye Luki, as they did in most places in Russia. Those Jews who had not fled before the town was occupied were arrested and then shot in the town square in October 1941.

Although Heeresgruppe Mitte resumed its eastwards advance with Operation *Typhoon*, it failed to capture Moscow and its forces were then left dangerously overextended as the Russian winter set in. Stavka gathered its remaining reserves and planned a multi-front winter counter-offensive to throw Heeresgruppe Mitte back on its heels. Several new 'shock armies' (*udarnaya armiya*) were formed to spearhead the counter-offensive. In late December 1941, the North-Western Front received the 3rd and 4th Shock armies and was tasked with smashing the left flank of Heeresgruppe Mitte. The 3rd Shock Army, under General-leytenant Maksim A. Purkayev, was ordered to seize Kholm and Velikiye Luki, while the 4th Shock Army would advance to capture Toropets, then push south towards Vitebsk. On the right flank, two other Soviet armies would move to encircle and destroy the German group in Demyansk. On the left flank, the Kalinin Front would attack the German 9.Armee at Rzhev. Stavka expected this operation to lead to rapid and decisive results.

On 7 January 1942, the Soviet North-Western Front winter counter-offensive began and achieved considerable success in its opening days because the Germans had so few forces deployed to defend the army-group boundaries. The Soviet 11th and 34th armies managed to isolate the German II.Armee-Korps in the Demyansk pocket, but a hastily organized Luftwaffe airlift prevented the garrison from collapsing. Likewise, Purkayev's 3rd Shock Army managed to encircle a small German garrison in Kholm, led by Generalmajor Theodor Scherer, but could not crush it, and the Luftwaffe dropped supplies to this force, as well (see Osprey Campaign 245: *Demyansk 1942–43*). The 4th Shock Army captured Toropets without much trouble, but the OKH scrambled to get a blocking force to Velikiye Luki and Velizh ahead of the Soviets. The only troops immediately available to defend Velikiye Luki were three battalions of *Landesschützen* from 403.Sicherungs-Division, which had its headquarters in Nevel.

As the crisis for Heeresgruppe Mitte unfolded, General der Infanterie Kurt von der Chevallerie's LIX.Armee-Korps – which had been on pleasant occupation duty in the La Rochelle region in France – was ordered to proceed post-haste to Vitebsk to take command of the jumble of ad hoc units on the army group's shattered left flank. Von der Chevallerie and his staff arrived in Vitebsk one week after the beginning of the Soviet winter counter-offensive, but had no formed units at hand. The OKH had ordered 218.Infanterie-Division, a Landwehr formation on coastal defence duty in Denmark, to move immediately to the Eastern Front by express rail. Incredibly, this division was split up between Heeresgruppe Nord and Heeresgruppe Mitte. Von der Chevallerie received only Infanterie-Regiment 323, an artillery battalion and a *Pionier-Kompanie* – which he sent to strengthen resistance at

German bicycle troops, advancing to Velikiye Luki, pass a destroyed Soviet ML-20 152mm howitzer, August 1941. The Red Army put up a tough fight for Velikiye Luki in July and August 1941 but lost the majority of the 22nd Army trying to hold the city. (Bundesarchiv, Bild 101I-267-0116-11, Foto: Friedrich)

Velikiye Luki – but another regiment went to reinforce the defence of Kholm and 16.Armee took the remainder of the division to form a reserve. Instead, the OKH promised von der Chevallerie another formation, 83.Infanterie-Division, which was en route from coastal duty in Normandy. The lead elements of 83.Infanterie-Division began arriving in Vitebsk on 15 January 1942, but it took a week for the bulk of the division to arrive.

The situation at the front was desperate, since the Soviets had ripped a huge 100km-wide hole in the boundary between the two German army groups. Consequently, von der Chevallerie was obliged to deploy 83.Infanterie-Division piecemeal as it arrived, to hold key terrain. Oberst Fritz Georg von Rappard's Infanterie-Regiment 277 and one artillery battalion was sent to reinforce the strongpoint at Velikiye Luki, but the rest of 83.Infanterie-Division was scattered across an 80km-wide front. Infanterie-Regiment 251 was sent to form a hedgehog around Polibino to defend the approaches to Nevel, while Oberst Adolf Sinzinger's Infanterie-Regiment 257 was sent to Velizh on the division's right flank. The 83. Infanterie-Division's headquarters moved to Nevel and this became the division's main supply base. Von der Chevallerie was informed that another division in France, 205.Infanterie-Division, was also earmarked for his LIX.Armee-Korps, but would not arrive until February. In addition, the OKH provided von der Chevallerie with three battalion-size specialist infantry formations: Jagd-Kommando 3, 7 and 11.

Thanks to the atrocious winter weather and their use of rail lines to rush troops to threatened sectors, von der Chevallerie was able to establish *Stützpunkte* (strongpoint) positions at all the key points just before the arrival of the 3rd and 4th Shock armies. Oberst Sinzinger's *Kampfgruppe* arrived in Velizh and was shocked to find that local security troops were more focused on rounding up Jews than putting the town into a state of defence. Sonderkommando 7a, an SS paramilitary unit, arrived shortly after Sinzinger with orders to eliminate 200 Jewish detainees in the city. Although Sinzinger was an ardent Austrian Nazi, he had no time for such nonsense; he ordered the SS personnel to leave Velizh, then released the 200 Jews and directed them to flee to the approaching Red Army. He then established a hedgehog defence in Velizh with his 3,000 troops, but he had very little artillery or supplies.

While the Soviet 'shock armies' sounded impressive on paper, at this point in the war they were seriously under-resourced and relied primarily on foot-marching infantry. Deep snow and supply deficiencies further reduced the mobility and firepower of these formations. Furthermore, Soviet operational-level commanders tried to pursue too many simultaneous objectives, which meant there was no real main effort. Adding to operational-level friction, the 3rd and 4th Shock armies were transferred from the North-Western Front to the Kalinin Front on 22 January 1942. Coordination between the two armies was negligible.

Von Rappard's Infanterie-Regiment 277 managed to hold Velikiye Luki without too much difficulty because Purkayev's 3rd Shock Army had no real numerical superiority in this sector and lacked the artillery to assault a fortified city. Purkayev committed the bulk of his army to capture Kholm – which he managed to surround on 21 January – but repeated attempts to capture the town failed. Initially, Purkayev sent only the 31st Rifle Brigade and one ski battalion towards Velikiye Luki, which was grossly insufficient to capture

Soviet infantry infiltrate through an obstacle. During the Soviet counter-offensive in the winter of 1941/42, the Red Army was able to encircle German units but failed to destroy them due to lack of adequate armour, artillery and air support. By the next winter, the Red Army was better equipped. (Nik Cornish at www. Stavka.org.uk)

the city. Instead, Purkayev's troops oozed around the garrison's open flanks and tried to cut the rail line to Nevel. Soviet partisans also appeared behind Velikiye Luki, further hindering German communications. Meanwhile, the 4th Shock Army made a major effort against Velizh, just 90km to the south. By 29 January, Kampfgruppe Sinzinger was surrounded in Velizh and threatened with annihilation. The Luftwaffe started a token airlift to supply Sinzinger's trapped garrison, but it was also conducting resupply operations for the Demyansk and Kholm pockets, as well. Von der Chevallerie was forced to commit all of the newly arriving 205.Infanterie-Division and part of the 330.Infanterie-Division to relieve Velizh and prevent the 4th Shock Army from reaching Vitebsk. It was a near-run thing and the 4th Shock Army came close to a major victory at Velizh. Another German garrison was surrounded in Demidov, south-east of Velizh. At one point, von der Chevallerie's staff had to help repel a Soviet attack on Zurazh, north of Vitebsk. Amazingly, Sinzinger brilliantly repulsed every assault by 4th Shock Army until von der Chevallerie was able to organize a relief operation. The LIX.Armee-Korps reopened ground communications to Velizh on 17 February and Demidov on 28 February. By the end of March 1942, it was clear that the Soviet winter counter-offensive in the Kholm–Velikiye Luki–Velizh sector had culminated without taking any of these objectives. Nevertheless, both shock armies continued attacking at Kholm and Velizh in April until their units were reduced to burnt-out shells. For the Germans, the lesson of the first Soviet winter counter-offensive was that encircled forces could hold onto fortified positions as long as the Luftwaffe could provide aerial resupply until a ground rescue mission could arrive. On the opposite side, Soviet commanders recognized the necessity for heavy artillery, tanks and engineer support to overcome enemy prepared positions.

After narrowly avoiding a catastrophic defeat, the Germans began to recover as spring approached. In April 1942, the Germans mounted a ground relief operation that achieved a link-up with the encircled forces in the Demyansk pocket and in early May, Scherer's encircled garrison in Kholm was also relieved. Adolf Sinzinger, after his successful defence of Velizh, was promoted and took command of 83.Infanterie-Division. Between 15 and 20 May, 83.Infanterie-Division mounted a local attack 20km south of Velikiye Luki, known as Operation *Schnepfenstrich* (*Snipe*), to clear two Soviet ski battalions off the road to Nevel. The road lay east of the main rail line, but Sinzinger wanted to push the Soviets as far back from his line of communications as possible. Operation *Schnepfenstrich* was a limited success; both Soviet battalions near Mart'yanovo were destroyed, but they managed to make the road unusable by demolishing bridges and laying plenty of mines. Furthermore, the 3rd Shock Army retaliated by mounting a counter-attack one week later with the 24th Rifle Division, which mauled the III./Infanterie-Regiment 251 and captured a hill overlooking the road. The 83.Infanterie-Division attacked on 30 May, again pushing the Soviets back from the road.

Unable to fully clear the road to Nevel, the garrison in Velikiye relied upon the rail line for its supplies. Sinzinger was provided with two armoured trains, *Panzerzug 3* and *27*, to assist with keeping the rail line open, but this proved problematic. Soviet partisans relentlessly harassed LIX.Armee-Korps' lines of communications, making it difficult to keep the garrison in Velikiye Luki in supply. During 1942, the Germans ran a supply train to Velikiye Luki once a week, escorted by one of the armoured trains. However, the partisans kept mining the rail lines and succeeded in damaging both armoured trains in late May. The rail bridge over the Lovat, 5km south-west of Velikiye Luki, was also damaged by partisans. Von der Chevallerie was obliged to conduct a number of anti-partisan operations between May and September 1942 to clear out enemy-infested areas behind his front lines.

The German command structure in the Velikiye Luki sector remained muddled throughout most of 1942. Initially, von der Chevallerie's LIX. Armee-Korps was assigned to 3.Panzer-Armee, but in April 1942, the corps was directly subordinated to Heeresgruppe Mitte and remained in that peculiar command arrangement for most of the year; this was the only German corps-size formation in 1942 that was not subordinate to an army headquarters. However, this command arrangement left LIX.Armee-Korps in a poor position to compete for resources with Heeresgruppe Mitte's other formations. Despite partially clearing the lines of communications to Velikiye Luki, its garrison remained in a precarious position. Sinzinger recognized that the garrison in Velikiye Luki was highly vulnerable to being isolated and took steps to prepare for a siege. With the help of construction troops, von Rappard's Infanterie-Regiment 277 began creating strongpoints all around Velikiye Luki and along its lines of communications.

On the other side of the line, the Kalinin Front took control over both the 3rd and 4th Shock armies in February 1942, but the front's resources were spread too thinly between the Kholm, Velikiye Luki and Velizh sectors. By the time that the winter counter-offensive culminated in March, Purkayev's 3rd Shock Army was gutted, having suffered over 40,000 casualties, including 15,000 dead or missing. Rather than reorganizing for another push against LIX.Armee-Korps, Stavka directed the Kalinin Front to use its remaining strength to assist with operations against the German 9.Armee in the Rzhev salient, which resulted in disaster: the 39th Army was encircled south-west of Rzhev and eventually destroyed by German counter-attacks. Following these events, neither the 3rd nor 4th Shock armies were capable of significant offensive action for months, and spent most of the summer of 1942 rebuilding. Consequently, the LIX.Armee-Korps sector was relatively quiet in June and July. It was not until August 1942 that the 3rd Shock Army received substantial reinforcements, in the form of the 2nd Guards Rifle Corps. Soon thereafter, Purkayev was promoted and took over the Kalinin Front, and General-major Kuzma N. Galitski was given command of the 3rd Shock Army. Galitski made some probing attacks in August and September to gauge the enemy defences, but nothing further happened. Despite the fact that the Velikiye Luki–Velizh sector was the most weakly held enemy

The Germans had a limited number of ski troops, who were used for patrolling and reconnaissance in the thinly held marsh areas that surrounded Velikiye Luki. During the winter of 1941/42, the German garrison in Velikiye Luki was not seriously threatened, because the 3rd Shock Army was mostly focused on reducing the Kholm pocket. (Nik Cornish at www. Stavka.org.uk)

sector on the entire Eastern Front, the Kalinin Front was not provided the manpower or material resources to make a major effort until 1942 was nearly over. Indeed, Stavka was so focused on other priorities for much of the year – relieving the siege of Leningrad, the Crimea, the Caucasus and Stalingrad – that the potential to achieve decisive results on the Kalinin Front was not properly recognized.

As autumn arrived, LIX.Armee-Korps was redesignated 'Gruppe Chevallerie' in October 1942, in acknowledgement of its semi-independent status. Since the OKH sent II.Luftwaffen-Feld-Korps with two *Luftwaffen-Feld-Divisionen* to hold the Velizh sector, von der Chevallerie was able to reduce the frontage held by his corps. The 83.Infanterie-Division reduced its sector in width, but was still forced to cover gaps between its three regiments with several security battalions.

After capturing the fortress of Sevastopol in July, Generalfeldmarschall Erich von Manstein's 11.Armee had been transferred to the Leningrad front, where the OKH hoped to use it in Operation *Nordlicht* (*Northern Lights*) to capture the city (see Osprey Campaign 215: *Leningrad 1941–44*). Instead, von Manstein's forces were used to repulse a major Soviet effort to relieve the city in the Second Battle of the Siniavino Heights, which lasted into October. Von Manstein achieved a tactical victory that blocked the Soviet relief attempt, but the season was now too late to launch a major offensive against Leningrad. On 25 October, Hitler called von Manstein to his forward headquarters at Vinnitsa to discuss options for the use of 11.Armee. Hitler was particularly concerned about the possibility of another Soviet winter counter-offensive, which he expected to be mounted against Heeresgruppe Mitte, not Heeresgruppe B at Stalingrad. Luftwaffe aerial reconnaissance had spotted large Soviet troop concentrations and armour gathering between Toropets and Kalinin, and the OKH correctly assessed that these forces would be used against 9.Armee in the Rzhev salient. Recognizing von Manstein's demonstrated skill at defeating Soviet offensives, Hitler ordered him to move his headquarters to Vitebsk and be prepared to cooperate with 9.Armee. The staff of Heeresgruppe Mitte had already issued a plan for a spoiling offensive towards Toropets, designated as Operation *Taubenschlag* (*Pigeon Shoot*). Now, von Manstein was expected to lead this operation if and when the Soviet offensive began. However, since 11.Armee had left most of its divisions under the command of Heeresgruppe Nord, von Manstein would need other units to fill out his command. Eventually, Heeresgruppe Nord agreed to release five divisions (8. and 12. Panzer divisions, 20.Infanterie-Division (mot.) and 93. and 291. Infanterie divisions) to 11.Armee, but dragged its feet on actually transferring the units. Likewise, the OKH agreed to transfer 3.Gebirgs-Division and some Nebelwerfer rocket artillery battalions to 11.Armee.

On 6 November, Gruppe Chevallerie was placed under von Manstein's command. Von Manstein tinkered with the *Taubenschlag* plan, claiming that

Strategic situation, 24 November 1942

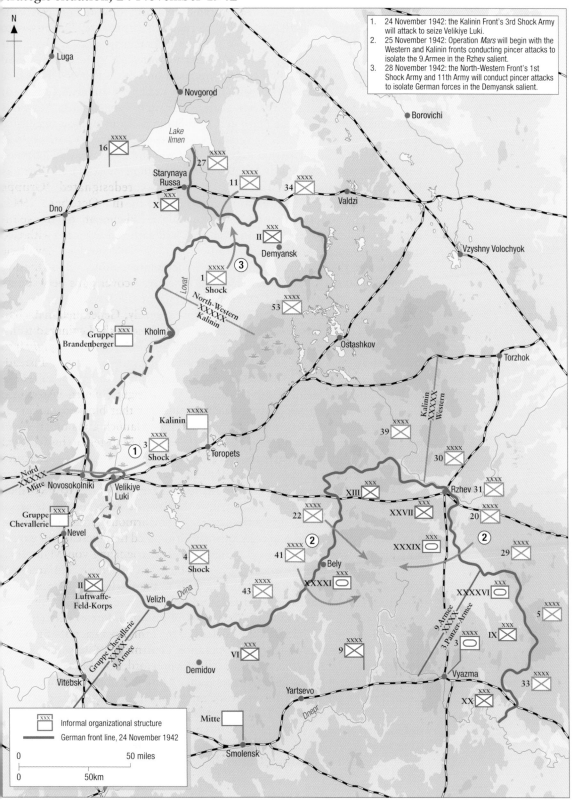

1. 24 November 1942: the Kalinin Front's 3rd Shock Army will attack to seize Velikiye Luki.
2. 25 November 1942: Operation *Mars* will begin with the Western and Kalinin fronts conducting pincer attacks to isolate the 9.Armee in the Rzhev salient.
3. 28 November 1942: the North-Western Front's 1st Shock Army and 11th Army will conduct pincer attacks to isolate German forces in the Demyansk salient.

Luga

Novgorod

Borovichi

Lake Ilmen

16

27

Starynaya Russa

11

34

Valdzi

Dno

X

II Demyansk

Vzyshny Volochyok

1 Shock

3

North-Western / Kalinin

53

Gruppe Brandenberger

Kholm

Ostashkov

Torzhok

Kalinin

39

Kalinin / Western

30

3 Shock

1

Toropets

Nord / Mitte

Novosokolniki

Velikiye Luki

XIII

Rzhev 31

XXVII

20

Gruppe Chevallerie

Nevel

22

2

XXXIX

2

29

4 Shock

41

2

Bely

XXXXI

II Luftwaffe-Feld-Korps

Velizh

Dvina

43

XXXXVI

5

Gruppe Chevallerie / 9.Armee

VI

9

9.Armee / 3.Panzer-Armee

IX

3

Vitebsk

Demidov

Vyazma

33

XX

Yartsevo

Dnepr

Mitte

Smolensk

	Informal organizational structure
	German front line, 24 November 1942

0 — 50 miles

0 — 50km

it could be accomplished with just 12.Panzer-Division, 3.Gebirgs-Division and 83.Infanterie-Division, even though none of these formations were near authorized strength. According to the revised plan for *Taubenschlag* von Manstein was expected to use Velikiye Luki as a springboard to attack eastwards with three divisions in order to seize Toropets, 65km away Gruppe Brandenburg would attack from Kholm with 8.Panzer-Division to assist the drive towards Toropets. It was an extremely ambitious plan and it took much longer to organize than anticipated. Nor did von Manstein show much interest in the plan, and the recent death of his son in combat was a further distraction. Nevertheless, by 18 November, 11.Armee had assembled 3.Gebirgs-Division in Novosokolniki and 291.Infanterie-Division and 12.Panzer-Division near Nevel. For the first time, most of 83.Infanterie-Division was concentrated near Velikiye Luki, leaving Gruppe Schröder and II.Luftwaffen-Feld-Korps to hold the rest of the front down to Velizh. Although the supply situation was minimal and not much Luftwaffe air support would be available, von Manstein had gathered sufficient forces to make Operation *Taubenschlag* feasible.

Although the OKH was expecting a Soviet winter counter-offensive, they completely miscalculated the scale and objectives of Stavka's operational plans. While the OKH did correctly assess that the Soviet Western and Kalinin fronts would launch a major offensive against 9.Armee in the Rzhev salient, Soviet resources were underestimated. After being on the ropes for most of 1942, Stavka was thinking big and planned to make all-out efforts in two separate regions. In addition to a major attack on 9.Armee in the Rzhev salient (designated as Operation *Mars*), Stavka planned to launch a surprise counter-offensive against the German 6.Armee at Stalingrad (Operation *Uranus*). In addition, supporting attacks would be made in other parts of the front, including the Demyansk and Velikiye Luki sectors. The Kalinin Front was reinforced so that it could participate in a series of front-level attacks that were intended to shatter the left wing of Heeresgruppe Mitte. Galitski's 3rd Shock Army was tasked with capturing Velikiye Luki and rupturing the fragile link between Heeresgruppe Mitte and Heeresgruppe Nord, which would assist the larger operation against the Rzhev salient. Luftwaffe aerial reconnaissance failed to detect the size of the Soviet build-up east of Velikiye Luki in mid-November, and consequently Gruppe Chevallerie did not expect a major attack by the 3rd Shock Army at this time.

On 19 November, Operation *Uranus* started in the south and achieved quick success. Within 24 hours, it was clear to the OKH that 6.Armee was in serious trouble and von Manstein and his staff were ordered to proceed to southern Russia to deal with that crisis. Without fanfare, 11.Armee was dissolved and redesignated as the nucleus of the new Heeresgruppe Don. All three of the divisions assigned to Operation *Taubenschlag* were ordered to proceed south by rail with von Manstein. Gruppe Chevallerie reverted to its semi-independent status under Heeresgruppe Mitte and now had to hurriedly reposition its remaining forces from an offensive posture to a defensive posture. On the night of 21/22 November, all three of the divisions began rail-loading to move south, and 83. Infanterie-Division shifted to occupy the front from Velikiye Luki to Chernosem station. The Soviet offensive, when it began, would catch Gruppe Chevallerie in transition.

CHRONOLOGY

1941

17 July   The German LVII.Armee-Korps (mot.) captures Velikiye Luki.

20 July   The Red Army recaptures Velikiye Luki – the first Russian city liberated.

26 August   The Germans recapture Velikiye Luki.

1942

7 January   The North-Western Front's winter counter-offensive begins. Purkayev's 3rd Shock Army attacks towards Velikiye Luki and Kholm.

15 January   Lead elements of 83.Infanterie-Division arrive in Vitebsk.

2 February   Infanterie-Regiment 277 arrives in Velikiye Luki.

20 May   German 83.Infanterie-Division conducts Operation *Schnepfenstrich*.

6 November   11.Armee assumes command over Gruppe Chevallerie.

11 November   Major Soviet air raid on Velikiye Luki.

21 November   11.Armee headquarters leaves Vitebsk to transfer to southern Russia.

24 November   Kalinin Front's winter offensive begins.

25 November   Operation *Mars* begins: the Kalinin and Western fronts attack the German 9.Armee in the Rzhev salient.

27 November   German garrison in Velikiye Luki is surrounded. Hitler orders the city held.

28 November   Galitski begins committing the 2nd Mechanized Corps into the battle. The Soviet North-Western Front attacks the German-held Demyansk salient.

29 November   The 8.Panzer-Division begins advancing towards Velikiye Luki from the north-west.

4 December   Gruppe Klatt links up with the encircled Gruppe Meyer.

13 December   First major Soviet attack on Velikiye Luki garrison.

14 December   Stützpunkt Hamburg is lost.

15 December   Gruppe Wöhler formed. Soviets demand surrender of Velikiye Luki.

17 December   First glider resupply mission into Velikiye Luki.

19 December   Gruppe Wöhler attacks towards Velikiye Luki.

21 December   Stützpunkt Bremen is lost.

23 December   Stützpunkt Bayreuth and the Felt Factory are lost.

1943

4 January   Operation *Totila* begins, and advances a few kilometres.

5 January   A Soviet attack from the north splits Velikiye Luki in two.

9 January   Major Günther Tribukait leads an armoured column that manages to reach the Citadel, but they are then trapped within the pocket.

16 January   Morning: Major Tribukait leads the breakout from the Citadel. Afternoon: The remainder of the German garrison in Velikiye Luki surrenders.

1946

1 February   Eight German POWs from the captured garrison are hanged in Velikiye Luki.

OPPOSING COMMANDERS

SOVIET

General-polkovnik Maksim A. Purkayev, commander of the Kalinin Front. With his pince-nez, Purkayev looked like a college professor and his career included diplomatic assignments, such as military attaché to Germany in the 1930s. He was well regarded as a staff officer – particularly by Zhukov – but lacked the kind of aggressive mindset that Stavka desired in front-level commanders. (Author's collection)

In the Red Army, decision-making resided in the front's military council, with the military represented by the front commander, Purkayev, and his chief of staff, Zakharov. However, the front's political officer, Dmitry S. Leonov (1899–1981), also had a voice in decision-making. In late 1942, group decision-making was still a dominant feature of the Red Army's command style.

General-polkovnik Maksim A. Purkayev (1894–1953) had been commander of the Kalinin Front since August 1942. Purkayev had been a conscript NCO in the Tsarist Army before joining the Red Army in 1918. During the Russo-Polish War in 1920 he was badly wounded. Later, Purkayev graduated from the Frunze Military Academy and served in several high-level staff assignments during the 1930s, including as military attaché to Germany in 1939 and 1940. At the outset of the war, Purkayev was Georgy Zhukov's chief of staff in the important Kiev Military District, but was relieved of his post in July 1941 and sent back to a training position in Moscow. Zhukov managed to get Purkayev command of the 3rd Shock Army, which he led during the Kholm–Demyansk operations. Notably, Purkayev failed to eliminate Scherer's surrounded garrison in Kholm. Nevertheless, Zhukov recommended him for command of the Kalinin Front for the upcoming Soviet winter counter-offensive. Purkayev was intelligent and a decent staff officer, but regarded as insufficiently aggressive as a tactical commander.

General-leytenant Matvey V. Zakharov (1898–1972) was appointed chief of staff of the Kalinin Front in January 1942. Zakharov was an early member of the Red Guards, and helped storm the Winter Palace in 1917. He was trained as an artilleryman and received General Staff training at the Frunze Military Academy in 1933. Zakharov proved to be a skilled staff officer who eventually rose to become a marshal of the Soviet Union.

General-major **Kuzma N. Galitski** (1897–1973) had been commander of the 3rd Shock Army since September 1942. Galitski was a career infantry officer who was steadily climbing in the Red Army until he was arrested by the NKVD during the purges in 1937. After ten months in prison, he was released and given command of a rifle division in the Russo-Finnish War. At the outset of the Russo-German War, Galitski's division was destroyed in the Minsk–Bialystok pocket in 1941, but he managed to escape and lead a rifle corps in the Battle of Smolensk. Galitski was badly wounded in August 1941 and spent nearly a year in recovery. Galitski had to carefully manage his resources during the Velikiye Luki operation, so that his forces could both repel all German relief attempts and have enough strength left to destroy the garrison in the city. Galitski's ability to coordinate air, artillery and ground attacks to keep Gruppe Wöhler off-balance during the later stages of the campaign was superb.

General-major Kuzma N. Galitski, commander of the 3rd Shock Army. A victim of the purges in 1937, Galitski staged a successful comeback at the start of the Russo-German War and proved himself a capable corps commander. During the Velikiye Luki campaign, he skilfully managed his forces to fend off one German relief attack after another, while the rest of his army crushed the enemy garrison in Velikiye Luki. (Author's collection)

General-major **Afanasy P. Beloborodov** (1903–90) was made commander of the 5th Guards Rifle Corps in October 1942. Beloborodov was of Siberian peasant stock and served as a teenage volunteer in the Red partisans during the Russian Civil War, but did not actually join the Red Army until 1923. As a junior infantry officer, he was awarded for valour in Manchuria and spent most of the interwar period stationed in the Far East. At the beginning of the war, Beloborodov was given command of the 78th Rifle Division (which became the 9th Guards Rifle Division), one of the first 'Siberian' divisions to reach the Western Front in November 1941. He led his division with distinction during the Moscow counter-offensive. Beloborodov was part of the Red Army's younger generation of commanders, who had moved up rapidly as a result of the purges and heavy losses in 1941.

General-major **Ivan P. Korchagin** (1898–1951) had been commander of the 2nd Mechanized Corps since September 1942. Korchagin was a former Tsarist infantry officer who was recruited into the Red Army in 1918. In 1937, he fell victim to the purges and spent 30 months in confinement by the NKVD. After his release, Korchagin was given command of one of the new tank divisions, which he led during the Battle of Smolensk in 1941. He spent much of 1942 in secondary roles until briefly commanding a tank corps in the summer of 1942. During the Velikiye Luki campaign, Korchagin's corps was never employed as a unified entity, but instead split up and used for a variety of offensive and defensive tasks.

General-major **Mikhail M. Gromov** (1899–1985) was appointed commander of the 3rd Air Army in May 1942. Gromov was originally trained as a pilot in 1918 and was something of an intellectual, which enabled him to serve in research roles in the Flight Research Institute for most of the interwar period. He was a talented test pilot and an aviation pioneer, establishing a long-distance flight record in 1937. However, Gromov had negligible command or combat experience at the start of World War II. Nevertheless, he was made commander of an aviation division on the Kalinin

General-major Afanasy P. Beloborodov, commander of the 5th Guards Rifle Corps. He led one of the few true 'Siberian divisions' in the 1941 Moscow counter-offensive and then became a corps commander in 1942. Beloborodov was part of the new generation of Soviet tactical commanders, who learned from the mistakes of 1941 and gradually honed their formations into effective combat teams. (Author's collection)

General der Infanterie Kurt von der Chevallerie, commander of LIX.Armee-Korps, or Gruppe Chevallerie. A competent, well-heeled professional soldier, von der Chevallerie had to plead for reinforcements to stave off disaster on his section of the front. (Author's collection)

Front in 1941–42 and moved up to command one of the first air armies Gromov was more of an aviation technocrat than an operational leader.

GERMAN

German decision-making was hindered by the imprecise command responsibility for the Velikiye Luki sector and the poor coordination between Heeresgruppe Nord and Heeresgruppe Mitte. Although Generalfeldmarschall Günther von Kluge's Heeresgruppe Mitte was responsible for Velikiye Luki, most of the force assigned to rescue the trapped garrison came from Heeresgruppe Nord.

General der Infanterie Kurt von der Chevallerie (1891–1945) became commander of LIX.Armee-Korps in December 1941. He was a Prussian infantryman of Huguenot descent, who came from a distinguished military family. Von der Chevallerie saw extensive front-line combat experience in World War I and served in the post-war Reichswehr. In the early years of World War II, he commanded 83.Infanterie-Division in the French campaign and 99.leichte.Infanterie-Division in southern Russia in 1941. Prior to the Soviet winter offensive at Velikiye Luki, von der Chevallerie underestimated enemy capabilities and his overconfidence resulted in tactical deployments that proved highly vulnerable. Throughout the Velikiye Luki campaign, von der Chevallerie was in an awkward command position that inhibited his ability to direct operations. He spent the

last half of the campaign watching Wöhler sacrifice his troops in futile attacks.

Generalleutnant Otto Wöhler (1894–1987) became chief of staff of Heeresgruppe Mitte at the start of the Soviet winter offensive. Wöhler was a career General Staff officer, having served in various army-level staff assignments between 1939 and 1942, but he had only limited command experience prior to the Battle of Velikiye Luki. In mid-December 1942, he was ordered by von Kluge to form an ad hoc command group to spearhead the relief effort for the encircled garrison in Velikiye Luki. From the beginning, Wöhler tried to conduct a methodical set-piece operation, which was unsuited to the terrain, weather, troops available and urgency of the relief mission. Wöhler was also handicapped in that he did not know the terrain or the troops under his command, which reduced him to the role of a resource manager, rather than combat leader.

Generalmajor Theodor Scherer (1889–1951) became commander of 83.Infanterie-Division on 7 November 1942. Scherer was a legend in the Wehrmacht after his epic 105-day defence of the Kholm pocket between January and May 1942. Scherer had been commissioned in the Bavarian Army and served in World War I, until he was captured by the British during the Battle of the Somme in July 1916. Returning to Germany after the war, Scherer left the army and joined the Bavarian police, serving from 1920 to 1935. When Hitler reinstated the draft and began enlarging the army, Scherer rejoined and became an infantry battalion commander in 1935 and then an infantry regiment commander in 1938. In June 1940, Scherer led his regiment during the assault crossing of the Marne River. As a commander, Scherer was a soldier's soldier, who inspired confidence in his men even under the most extreme conditions. However, he was extremely frustrated by the situation handed to him at Velikiye Luki and his inability to save the trapped garrison.

Generalleutnant Erich Brandenberger (1892–1955) commanded 8.Panzer-Division at Velikiye Luki. Brandenberger served as an artillery officer in the Bavarian Army in World War I and in the post-war Reichswehr. At the start of World War II, he served in staff roles in France but was given command of 8.Panzer-Division in 1941, even though he had no major command experience. By late 1942, Brandenberger was an experienced commander and although he was not the most aggressive Panzer commander, he was able to keep his very depleted division in the fight for the entire Velikiye Luki campaign.

Oberstleutnant Eduard Heinrich Hartwig Reinhard Freiherr von Sass (1900–46) became commander of Grenadier-Regiment 277, 83.Infanterie-Division in October 1942. Von Sass was the son of a Berlin lawyer and studied law himself before joining the Reichswehr in 1924. His family had ancestral ties to Estonia and minor nobility in East Prussia. Prior to the siege of Velikiye Luki, von Sass had negligible front-line command experience, and he was an odd choice to replace the very experienced Oberst Fritz Georg von

Generalleutnant Otto Wöhler, chief of staff of Heeresgruppe Mitte, was tasked by von Kluge with directing the relief of the trapped garrison in Velikiye Luki. Wöhler was a classic German General Staff-trained officer, but his methodical methods proved unsuited to the task of launching a hasty rescue mission. (Author's collection)

Generalmajor Theodor Scherer took command of 83.Infanterie-Division just 18 days before the Soviet offensive started. The 'hero of Kholm' had to watch in frustration as part of his division was destroyed in Velikiye Luki while the rest was bled dry in the relief effort. (Author's collection)

Rappard. During the siege, von Sass was hard-pressed to maintain his command and was criticized by his superiors for not providing detailed reports on his situation. Nevertheless, in order to boost his flagging morale, he was promoted to *Oberst* and awarded the Ritterkreuz des Eisernen Kreuzes during the siege. Some men rise to the occasion during desperate sieges – Gordon at Khartoum, Chard at Rorke's Drift, Scherer at Kholm – von Sass was not one of those men.

Generaloberst Robert Ritter von Greim (1892–1945) had commanded Luftwaffenkommando Ost since April 1942. Von Greim joined the Bavarian Army in 1911 and served in the opening stages of World War I as a junior artillery officer before switching to the aviation service in 1915. Von Greim had a very successful career as a fighter pilot between 1917 and 1918, achieving 28 victories, which gained the award of the Pour le Mérite. After the war, he became an early follower of Hitler, joining the Nazi Party and participating in the failed 1923 Beer Hall Putsch. In return, von Greim played a critical role in the creation of the Luftwaffe between 1933 and 1937. At the start of World War II, he commanded 5.Flieger-Division in the Polish campaign. Between 1940 and 1942, he led V.Fliegerkorps. By late 1942, von Greim was a highly experienced front-line aviation commander, but the resources he commanded were inadequate for the missions assigned.

Generalleutnant Erich Brandenberger, commander of 8.Panzer-Division, struggles with the mud in Russia, along with his troops. By 1942, Brandenberger had seen quite a lot of Russian mud and realized that a winter rescue operation with extemporized forces would be extremely difficult. (Süddeutsche Zeitung Bild 00109985, Foto: Scherl)

OPPOSING FORCES

SOVIET

By mid-November 1942, the Soviet 3rd Shock Army was far more of a combined-arms formation than it had been during the first winter campaign. Reinforced with veteran Guards rifle units, tanks and heavy artillery, the 3rd Shock Army had gained a significant edge over Gruppe Chevallerie in terms of numbers and firepower. Overall, the 3rd Shock Army had a strength of 96,000 troops, of which about 50 per cent were committed to the initial attacks. However, the material condition of the front-line troops was inadequate in terms of food and clothing, and Stavka did not provide the logistical resources for a protracted battle at Velikiye Luki. Galitski's 3rd Shock Army headquarters was located in the village of Yarmishenki, 15km south-east of Velikiye Luki.

Infantry

The main strike force within the 3rd Shock Army was provided by General-major Afanasy P. Beloborodov's 5th Guards Rifle Corps, which had three attached rifle divisions (9th Guards Rifle Division, 46th Guards Rifle Division and 357th Rifle Division), and the 21st Guards Rifle Division. Stavka had formed 11 Guards rifle corps between December 1941 and August 1942,

A Soviet Maxim machine-gunner and riflemen provide overwatch for friendly infantry advancing in the streets of Velikiye Luki. Note the heavily shell-damaged building behind them. Also note that the troops are not equipped with much in the way of winter kit beyond their Ushanka hats and padded jackets – no gloves. The troops of the 3rd Shock Army suffered from shortages of food and clothing due to poorly managed rear services. (Author's collection)

A Soviet 82mm PM-41 mortar team drills in the snow. The 82mm mortar was the primary battalion-level fire support asset and was useful to support urban assaults as well as defensive missions. Incredibly, the Soviet Union built over 100,000 82mm mortars in 1942. (Courtesy of the Central Museum of the Armed Forces, Moscow via Stavka)

and these formations were intended to provide a solid core of veteran infantry for any offensive operation. While the Guards rifle units were combat-experienced formations, at this point in the war they did not have much better equipment or training than the standard rifle units; most divisions were short of support weapons and even basic field gear. Indeed, it would be more apt to describe the Guards rifle troops of the Kalinin Front as solid, rather than elite. Typically, a Guards rifle division had about 8,000 troops in the field at the start of an operation, while regular rifle divisions had about 6,500 troops. In October 1942, Soviet infantry doctrine was revised and required divisions to attack in a single echelon on a 4–5km-wide front, in order to maximize combat power in the initial stage of an attack. The Red Army was also beginning to experiment with urban warfare tactics, and Velikiye Luki would be the first test; instead of relying upon large formations, the 3rd Shock Army intended to use company-size assault detachments, reinforced by sappers and supported by a few tanks.

Armour

Throughout most of 1942, the only armoured support the Kalinin Front could provide the 3rd Shock Army was the 184th Tank Brigade (equipped with American-made M3 Lee tanks) and two separate tank battalions (equipped with a mix of M3 Lees and T-60 light tanks). These infantry support tank units had typically been used in company strength to support local operations. Just prior to the beginning of the Velikiye Luki operation, Stavka provided the 3rd Shock Army with its first large mechanized formation from the RVGK (*Rezerv Verkhovnogo Glavnokomandovaniya* – Stavka Reserve): General-major Ivan P. Korchagin's 2nd Mechanized Corps. The 2nd Mechanized Corps was a powerful formation, equipped with 215 tanks, including 10 KV-1 heavy tanks and 117 T-34 medium tanks. However, in order to reach the Kalinin Front's assembly areas in time for the operation, 2nd Mechanized Corps was required to move 400km on its own tracks, which resulted in 54 tanks and 300 vehicles falling out with mechanical defects. Due to a shortage of spare parts, 2nd Mechanized Corps would not be fully operational at the start of the offensive, and it was still in an assembly area 15km south-east of Velikiye Luki. During the early stage of the offensive, Galitski used small groups of tanks in the infantry support role, and he ended up committing 2nd Mechanized Corps in piecemeal fashion, which reduced its impact upon the campaign. Once involved in city fighting, Soviet tanks proved highly vulnerable to German anti-tank guns, but the Red Army had one trick up its sleeve: the KV-8 heavy flame-thrower tank, which was nearly impervious to the lighter German anti-tank weapons.

A Soviet ML-20 152mm howitzer. Galitski's 3rd Shock Army was provided with several regiments of 152mm howitzers and this was his main long-range striking power. Typically, the ML-20 could hurl a 40kg HE shell out to 17km. Heavy artillery played a major role in the Soviet victory at Velikiye Luki. (Nik Cornish at www. Stavka.org.uk)

Artillery

Purkayev had about 400 artillery pieces to support his offensive, including 20 120mm heavy mortars and 96 multiple rocket-launchers (BM-8). The 3rd Shock Army's main punch was provided by two Guards artillery regiments, equipped with 152mm ML-20 howitzers. However, the Soviet artillery regiments were dispersed among individual assault groups instead of concentrated into larger artillery units under centralized control – a mistake that would be rectified in later campaigns. The 3rd Shock Army did have the firepower to reduce German strongpoints, although its artillery units had difficulty massing fires against important targets, and still tended to rely upon barrage fire. As the Velikiye Luki operation progressed, the Soviet superiority in artillery played a major role in halting German relief efforts and reducing the encircled German garrison.

Air support

General-major Mikhail M. Gromov's 3rd Air Army (*Vozdushnaya armiya*) was formed in May 1942, but it suffered badly during air battles with the Luftwaffe in the summer of 1942 and was rendered nearly combat-ineffective. In mid-November 1942, Gromov received substantial reinforcements in the shape of the 1st and 2nd Fighter Aviation corps, 1st Assault Aviation Corps and the 1st Bomber Corps, as well as a few elite Guards aviation regiments. At the start of the winter counter-offensive, the 3rd Air Army had about 1,100 aircraft, which gave it a roughly 10:1 superiority over the opposing Luftwaffenkommando Ost. However, Gromov had to split his resources between the Velikiye Luki,

The 3rd Air Army had six regiments' worth of Pe-2 bombers in the 1st Bomber Aviation Corps, with a total of over 150 aircraft. Overall, the Pe-2 was a good light bomber, which could deliver up to four FAB-250 bombs. During the Battle of Velikiye Luki, 3rd Air Army used its Pe-2s to bomb the German garrison on a regular basis – the first time that a single German regiment had been the target of so much aerial firepower. (Author's collection)

A Soviet officer briefs crewmen in an Il-2 Sturmovik unit. Note the significant age differences among the crewmen and the muddy nature of their forward airstrip. The Soviet war machine was more geared to operate under primitive field conditions than the Wehrmacht, which paid off during the harsh winter campaigns of 1941/42 and 1942/43. (Author's collection)

Velizh and Rzhev sectors, meaning that 3rd Shock Army typically only received about 30 per cent of 3rd Air Army's daily sorties.

The 3rd Air Army had 11 fighter regiments, each with roughly 30 aircraft; two equipped with the Yak-1, four with the Yak-7B, one with the British-built Hurricane and four with the new La-5. The La-5 was a good match against the Bf-109Fs that patrolled this sector, although the Germans still had the edge in pilot experience and training. Gromov's real striking power resided in the 1st Assault Aviation Corps (*Aviatsionnyi Shturmovoy Korpus*), which had over 300 Il-2 Sturmovik ground-attack aircraft, and the 1st Bomber Aviation Corps (*Bombardirovochnaya Aviatsionnyi Korpus*) with 180 Pe-2 bombers. The single regiment of Tu-2 bombers was used to strike targets further in the rear, such as rail yards. Gromov also had a large collection of light night bombers (U-2, R-5 and Po-5) to harass the Germans during the long hours of darkness. For the first time in the Russian campaign, the Soviet Air Force (*Voyenno-Vozdushnye Sily*) could provide the Red Army with significant air support in a major offensive.

Logistics

The 3rd Shock Army's logistical situation was not particularly favourable at the start of the operation, since plans for the offensive had been rushed, and much of the Kalinin Front's efforts went to support the units involved in Operation *Mars*. Nor did it help that General-major Arkadiy

The Kalinin Front's logistic situation was extremely primitive and front-line units were particularly short of food. In winter, horse-drawn sleds were used to deliver bread to forward areas. Stavka eventually relieved several rear-area commanders in January 1943, when it recognized that logistic shortages were playing a role in slowing down the pace of Soviet operations. (Courtesy of the Central Museum of the Armed Forces, Moscow via Stavka)

P. Golubev, commander of the 3rd Shock Army's rear services, was incompetent and not responsive to dealing with problems. The supply of fuel and ammunition was adequate for a short-term offensive, but no more. The main issue affecting the troops of 3rd Shock Army was serious shortages of food and lack of basic hygienic facilities, which meant that the front-line troops started the operation hungry, tired and dirty. Even in the Guards units, some of the troops were still wearing summer cotton uniforms, instead of winter uniforms. Oftentimes, food and other supplies were available somewhere in the rear, but Golubev's rear-area service troops did not ensure that they reached front-line troops. General-major Petr E. Smokachev, commander of the Kalinin Front's support services, claimed that he was unaware of the shortages and supply problems affecting 3rd Shock Army. Eventually, Stavka recognized that the Kalinin Front's supply services were less than efficient and removed both Smokachev and Golubev, but not until the Velikiye Luki operation was nearly over.

German front-line infantry, winter 1942/43. Unlike the previous winter, the Germans were better equipped with winter clothing and suffered fewer cold-weather casualties. However, when a rainy period with near-freezing temperatures occurred in mid-December 1942, Gruppe Wöhler experienced a large number of frostbite casualties, which contributed to the failure of the first relief attempt. (Nik Cornish at www.Stavka.org.uk)

GERMAN

On 23 November 1942, the main infantry units in Gruppe Chevallerie consisted of 83.Infanterie-Division, three *Jäger-Bataillonen* and three security battalions. Some elements of 3.Gebirgs-Division and 291.Infanterie-Division – which were in the process of moving out of the region by rail – were still available, but not assigned to Gruppe Chevallerie.

Infantry

The 83.Infanterie-Division was part of the 6.Welle (6th Wave), raised from reservists in December 1939. The division performed well in the campaigns in Poland and France, but missed Operation *Barbarossa* and was deployed piecemeal into combat on the Eastern Front in January 1942. During the winter fighting for Velikiye Luki and Velizh, 83.Infanterie-Division suffered significant casualties, and by June 1942, it was forced to disband one infantry battalion from each of its three infantry regiments (which were all redesignated as Grenadier regiments in October 1942), leaving it with a total of six infantry battalions. In Oberstleutnant Freiherr von Sass' Grenadier-Regiment 277, responsible for defending Velikiye Luki, the two remaining battalions had 83–86 per cent of their authorized ration strength prior to the Soviet offensive: Hauptmann Erich Darnedde's I./Grenadier-Regiment 277 with 740 men and Major Schwabe's II./Grenadier-Regiment 277 with 719 men. Von Sass also had his regimental anti-tank company (14./Grenadier-Regiment 277), one company from another regiment (5./Grenadier-Regiment

A pair of Luftwaffe He 111 bombers at a forward airfield. The ability of the Luftwaffe to support ground troops was significantly reduced by the winter weather, although Kampfgeschwader 53 flew nearly 200 aerial resupply missions over Velikiye Luki. The Luftwaffe also created a forward airstrip on the frozen Great Ivan Lake, west of the city. (Nik Cornish at www. Stavka.org.uk)

257) and one security battalion. The troops of Grenadier-Regiment 277 and both security battalions were partly equipped with captured foreign weapons (Czech, French and Russian), including one-third of their machine guns and a significant portion of their small arms. Major Wilhelm Sonnewald, the Ortskommandant (city commander), was in charge of the security troops, Feldgendarmerie (military police) and some other support troops in the city. Altogether, the German garrison in Velikiye Luki possessed fewer than 3,000 combat troops (battle strength, or *Gefechtstärke*), which was insufficient to hold a 22km-long perimeter defence for very long.

Gruppe Meyer (based on Grenadier-Regiment 257) was the nearest friendly force to Velikiye Luki at the start of the campaign, located 10km to the south-west. However, Gruppe Meyer only had two infantry battalions with a total of just 1,300 infantrymen and one battalion of artillery with 12 howitzers. Just before the Soviet offensive, Scherer reinforced Meyer with a battery of ten assault guns from Sturmgeschütz-Abteilung 183, a Panzerjäger detachment with 12 anti-tank guns, a Flak detachment with three 8.8cm guns and two batteries of 15cm Nebelwerfer. Nevertheless, Gruppe Meyer was seriously short of ammunition and was hard-pressed just to maintain the Nevel–Velikiye Luki rail connection. Throughout the campaign, the Germans were consistently short of infantry, which hampered their ability to hold terrain.

The right flank of 83.Infanterie-Division was guarded by Gruppe Schröder (three battalions), which altogether amounted to about 1,800 troops. Gruppe Schröder benefitted from occupying prepared defensive positions, but its two security battalions were equipped primarily with captured Czech and Russian weapons and had limited firepower. Jäger-Bataillon 3 and Jäger-Bataillon 5 were light infantry units, primarily intended for anti-partisan operations, but the troops were of higher quality than the security units. The fact that Gruppe Chevallerie was forced to use security battalions to hold its front line for extended periods is indicative of how hard-pressed the Germans were for manpower in this sector.

Artillery and anti-tank support

The 83.Infanterie-Division's defence rested upon artillery and anti-tank firepower, although ammunition shortages plagued the Germans throughout the campaign. Inside Velikiye Luki, von Sass had quite a lot of artillery support for a regiment: two howitzer batteries from the III./Artillerie-Regiment 183 (with nine 10.5cm leFH 18), one howitzer battery with three 15cm sFH 18 howitzers, one cannon battery from Artillerie-Regiment 70 (with three 10cm sK 18) and a heavy mortar battery with three 21cm Mörser from Artillerie-Regiment 76. Altogether, these 18 artillery pieces – directed by observers from the leichte Beobachtungs-Abteilung 17 – could hit targets anywhere on the defensive perimeter. In addition, von Sass had 22 Nebelwerfer rocket-launchers (eight 15cm and 14 28cm/32cm) and his

infantry had 12 8cm mortars and two 7.5cm infantry guns; these short-range weapons could prove devastating in breaking up enemy assaults that were caught in the open. Also, a battery of 12 2cm light Flak guns were useful for air defence or repelling ground assaults. Nevertheless, the German artillery in Velikiye Luki was handicapped by a limited ammunition stockpile and could only receive token amounts by air. Furthermore, the artillery in Velikiye Luki had very limited mobility, which meant that they had to fight a static battle – once their positions were discovered, they would be relentlessly pounded by the enemy.

One of the lessons of the defence of Kholm was that encircled garrisons could only survive if they possessed strong anti-tank defences. Von Sass started the battle with a total of 24 anti-tank guns (13 3.7cm Pak, four 5cm Pak 38, two 7.5cm Pak 97/38 and five ex-Soviet 45mm guns), which meant that each company sector only had a single anti-tank gun. The 3.7cm anti-tank guns were usually ineffective against Soviet T-34 tanks, but von Sass' regiment had been provided with about 100 of the new Stielgranate 41 HEAT rounds, which could theoretically enable the 3.7cm Pak to knock out a T-34. Von Sass' 5cm Pak 38 anti-tank guns were also equipped with about 150 Panzergranate 40 tungsten-core rounds, which were very effective against T-34s. At the start of the campaign, German anti-tank capabilities in Velikiye Luki were adequate, but the Soviets rapidly became adept at picking off German anti-tank gunners. By late December, German Panzerjäger became a priority target for the enemy and von Sass had to keep requesting new anti-tank guns and gunners be delivered by glider.

The rest of 83.Infanterie-Division was also equipped with a variety of anti-tank and artillery pieces, ranging from the obsolete 3.7cm Pak to the excellent 7.5cm Pak 40. Gruppe Meyer (Grenadier-Regiment 257) was reinforced with a battery of assault guns just prior to the Soviet offensive. The 83.Infanterie-Division was also obliged to provide Gruppe Schröder with two batteries of artillery and ten anti-tank guns, which dispersed some of the division's firepower in a non-critical sector.

ORDER OF BATTLE, 24 NOVEMBER 1942

SOVIET

KALININ FRONT (GENERAL-POLKOVNIK MAKSIM A. PURKAYEV)

3rd Shock Army (General-major Kuzma N. Galitski)
Northern Attack Group
381st Rifle Division (Polkovnik Boris S. Maslov)
    1259th, 1261st and 1263rd Rifle regiments
31st Rifle Brigade (Podpolkovnik Aleksandr. V. Yakushev)
Central Attack Group
5th Guards Rifle Corps (General-major Afanasy P. Beloborodov)
    9th Guards Rifle Division (General-major Ignatiy V. Prostiakov)
        18th, 22nd, 31st Guards Rifle regiments
        36th Separate Tank Regiment [23 T-34, 16 T-70]
    46th Guards Rifle Division (General-major Sergei I. Karapetian)
        494th, 508th and 628th Guards Rifle regiments
        34th Separate Tank Regiment [23 T-34, 16 T-70]
    357th Rifle Division (Polkovnik Aleksandr L. Kronik)
        1188th, 1190th and 1192nd Rifle regiments
        27th Separate Tank Regiment [23 T-34, 16 T-70]
        385th Guards Artillery Regiment [12 152mm]
    41st Guards Artillery Regiment [122mm/152mm]
    289th Engineer Battalion
257th Rifle Division (Polkovnik Anatoly A. Dyakonov)
    943rd, 948th and 953rd Rifle regiments
21st Guards Rifle Division (General-major Denis V. Mikhailov)
    59th, 64th and 69th Guards Rifle regiments
Southern Attack Group
28th Rifle Division (Polkovnik Sergei A. Kniazkov)
    88th, 144th and 235th Rifle regiments
184th Tank Brigade (Podpolkovnik Stepan A. Sevastyanov) [30 M3 Lee, 16 T-60]
Reserve
2nd Mechanized Corps (General-major Ivan P. Korchagin)
    18th, 34th and 43rd Mechanized brigades [each brigade has 23 T-34, 16 T-70]
    33rd and 36th Tank brigades [each brigade has five KV-1, 24 T-34, 20 T-70]
    33rd Armoured Car Battalion
    68th Motorcycle Battalion
    79th Anti-Tank Artillery Regiment
[Total for 2nd Mechanized Corps: ten KV-1, 117 T-34, 88 T-70 = 215 tanks]
Front assets
146th and 170th Independent Tank battalions [mixed: M3 Lee, T-60]
38th Guards Artillery Regiment [122mm/152mm]
270th, 613th, 1094th and 1190th Artillery regiments
61st and 304th Guards Mortar regiments
43rd, 106th, 107th, 205th, 240th and 410th Guards Mortar battalions
603rd Mortar Regiment
171st, 316th, 389th and 699th Anti-Tank regiments
582nd and 609th Anti-Aircraft Artillery regiments
225th, 288th and 293rd Engineer battalions
3rd Air Army (General-major Mikhail M. Gromov)
1st Fighter Aviation Corps (General-mayor Evgeniy M. Beletskiy)
    210th Fighter Aviation Division

        32nd Guards Fighter Aviation Regiment [Yak-7B]
        169th Fighter Aviation Regiment [La-5]
    274th Fighter Aviation Division
        271st Fighter Aviation Regiment [Yak-1]
        653rd Fighter Aviation Regiment [Yak-1]
        875th Fighter Aviation Regiment [Yak-7]
2nd Fighter Aviation Corps (General-mayor Aleksei S. Blagoveshchenskiy)
    209th Fighter Aviation Division
        1st Guards Fighter Aviation Regiment [Yak-7B]
        12th Fighter Aviation Regiment [Yak-7B]
    215th Fighter Aviation Division
        2nd Guards Fighter Aviation Regiment [La-5]
        263rd Fighter Aviation Regiment [La-5]
        522nd Fighter Aviation Regiment [La-5]
    256th Fighter Aviation Division
        157th Fighter Aviation Regiment [Hurricane]
1st Assault Aviation Corps (General-mayor Vasily G. Ryazanov)
    264th Assault Aviation Division
        235th Assault Aviation Regiment [Il-2]
        451st Assault Aviation Regiment [Il-2]
        809th Assault Aviation Regiment [Il-2]
    266th Assault Aviation Division
        66th Assault Aviation Regiment [Il-2]
        673rd Assault Aviation Regiment [Il-2]
        735th Assault Aviation Regiment [Il-2]
    292nd Assault Aviation Division
        667th Assault Aviation Regiment [Il-2]
        800th Assault Aviation Regiment [Il-2]
        820th Assault Aviation Regiment [Il-2]
212th Assault Aviation Division
    671st Assault Aviation Regiment [Il-2]
    685th Assault Aviation Regiment [Il-2]
    687th Assault Aviation Regiment [Il-2]
1st Bomber Aviation Corps (General-mayor Vladimir A. Sudets)
    263rd Bomber Aviation Division
        46th Bomber Aviation Regiment [Pe-2]
        202nd Bomber Aviation Regiment [Pe-2]
        321st Bomber Aviation Regiment [Pe-2]
    293rd Bomber Aviation Division
        780th Bomber Aviation Regiment [Pe-2]
        804th Bomber Aviation Regiment [Pe-2]
        854th Bomber Aviation Regiment [Pe-2]
6th Guards Assault Aviation Regiment [Il-2]
132nd Bomber Regiment [Tu-2]
11th Separate Reconnaissance Regiment [Pe-2]
648th Night Bomber Aviation Regiment [U-2]
695th Night Bomber Aviation Regiment [U-2]
887th Night Bomber Aviation Regiment [R-5]
930th Night Bomber Aviation Regiment [Po-5]
195th Mixed Aviation Regiment [U-2]
881st Mixed Aviation Regiment [U-2]
882nd Mixed Aviation Regiment [U-2]
883rd Mixed Aviation Regiment [U-2]

SOVIET REINFORCEMENTS

2 December 1942
44th Ski Brigade (Polkovnik Pavel. F. Lobov)
45th Ski Brigade (Podpolkovnik Anatoly I. Serebryakov)
26th Rifle Brigade
13 December 1942
8th Estonian Rifle Corps (General-major Lembit A. Pärn)
    7th Estonian Rifle Division (Polkovnik Augustus A. Vassil)
        27th Rifle Regiment

        300th Rifle Regiment
        354th Rifle Regiment
    249th Estonian Rifle Division (Polkovnik Arthur-Alexander I. Saueselg)[1]
        917th Rifle Regiment
        921st Rifle Regiment

1   Relieved of command on 29 December 1942.

925th Rifle Regiment
19th Guards Rifle Division (General-major David M. Baranov)
    54th Rifle Regiment
    56th Rifle Regiment
    61st Guards Rifle Regiment
37th Separate Tank Regiment [23 T-34, 16 T-70]
38th Separate Tank Regiment [23 T-34, 16 T-70]
45th Separate Tank Regiment [23 T-34, 16 T-70]

9 December 1942
2nd Tank Brigade (Polkovnik Nikolai B. Martynov) [45 M3 Lee and M3 Stuart]

0 December 1942
5th Ski Brigade

1 December 1942
15th Flame-thrower Tank Battalion [14 KV-8]

2 December 1942
60th Rifle Division (Polkovnik Viktor G. Pozniak)
    1193rd Rifle Regiment

1195th Rifle Regiment
1197th Rifle Regiment
100th Kazakh Rifle Brigade (Podpolkovnik Efim V. Voronkov)[2]

25 December 1942
47th Mechanized Brigade (Podpolkovnik Ivan F. Dremov)

5 January 1943
28th Independent Engineer Battalion

8 January 1943
32nd Rifle Division (Polkovnik Ivan S. Bezugly)
    17th Rifle Regiment
    113th Rifle Regiment
    322nd Rifle Regiment

15 January 1943
150th Rifle Division (Polkovnik Nikolay O. Guz)
    469th Rifle Regiment
    674th Rifle Regiment
    856th Rifle Regiment

2   Killed in action, early January 1943.

GERMAN

HEERESGRUPPE MITTE (GENERALFELDMARSCHALL GÜNTHER VON KLUGE)

Gruppe Chevallerie (General der Infanterie Kurt von der Chevallerie)
83.Infanterie-Division (Generalmajor Theodor Scherer)
Gruppe Giehl (Oberstleutnant Johann Giehl)
    II./Grenadier-Regiment 251
    I./Artillerie-Regiment 183 (less 1.Batterie)
Gruppe Meyer (Oberstleutnant Constantin Meyer)
    I., II./Grenadier-Regiment 257 (less one company)
    III./Grenadier-Regiment 251
    II./Artillerie-Regiment 183
    3./Sturmgeschütz-Abteilung 185 [seven StuG III, five StuH 42]
., II./Grenadier-Regiment 277 (Oberstleutnant Freiherr von Sass)
    14./Grenadier-Regiment 277
    5./Grenadier-Regiment 257
Sicherungs-Bataillon 336
    1., 3./Pionier-Bataillon 183
Feld-Ausbildung-Bataillon 183
III./Artillerie-Regiment 183 [nine 10.5cm l.FH 18, three 15cm s.FH 18]
4.Batterie./Artillerie-Regiment 70 [three 10cm sK 18]
2.Mörser-Batterie, Artillerie-Regiment 736 [three 21cm]
Stab., 9./Werfer-Lehr-Regiment 1 [eight 15cm Nebelwerfer]
I./schweres Werfer-Regiment 3 [14 28cm/32cm Nebelwerfer]
3./Heeres-Flakartillerie-Abteilung 286 (mot.) [12 2cm FlaK]

1./leichte Flak-Abteilung 93 (mot.) [Luftwaffe] [3.7cm FlaK]
Gruppe Schröder
Sicherungs-Bataillon 591
Sicherungs-Bataillon 795
Jäger-Bataillon 5
Jäger-Bataillon 3
Sicherungs-Bataillon 343
Forces in or near Novosokolniki, Senkina Gora
3.Gebirgs-Division
    Gruppe Klatt (Oberst Paul Klatt)
        II., III./Gebirgsjäger-Regiment 138
        11./Infanterie-Regiment 251
        1./Artillerie-Regiment 183
Sicherungs-Bataillon 663
II./schweres Werfer-Regiment 3 [28cm/32cm Nebelwerfer]
IV./Artillerie-Regiment 183 [15cm]

LUFTWAFFE

Luftwaffenkommando Ost (General der Flieger Robert Ritter von Greim)
2.Flieger-Division (Generalleutnant Johannes Fink)
    Stab, IV./Jagdgeschwader 51 [41 Bf 109F]
    III./Sturzkampfgeschwader 77 [32 Ju 87B/R]
    I./Kampfgeschwader 1 [28 Ju 88]
    2.(H)/23 [six Hs 126B]
III./Jagdgeschwader 54 [Bf 109G]

GERMAN REINFORCEMENTS

25 November 1942
I., II./Kampfgeschwader 53 (Oberst Karl-Eduard Wilke) [35 He 111H]
27–29 November 1942
Gruppe Jaschke
    20.Infanterie-Division (mot.) (Generalmajor Erich Jaschke)
        I., II./Grenadier-Regiment (mot.) 76
        I., II., III./Grenadier-Regiment (mot.) 90
        II., III./Artillerie-Regiment 20 [10.5cm/15cm]
        I., II./Werfer-Lehr-Regiment 1 [eight 15cm Nebelwerfer]
        6./schweres Werfer-Regiment 3 [14 28cm/32cm Nebelwerfer]
    291.Infanterie-Division (Generalleutnant Werner Göritz)
        I., II./Grenadier-Regiment 505 (Oberst Wilhelm Hesse)
        II., IV./Artillerie-Regiment 291 [10.5cm/15cm]
        III./Werfer-Regiment 55 [18 15cm]
        II./Artillerie-Regiment 47 [four 10cm/eight 15cm]

Gruppe Häheler
    III./Grenadier-Regiment (mot.) 76
    III./Grenadier-Regiment 506
    8./Panzer-Regiment 29 [12.Panzer-Division]
Jäger-Bataillon 1
1., 2./Sturmgeschütz-Abteilung 185 (Hauptmann Horst Krafft) [13 StuG III, four StuH 42]
Sturmgeschütz-Batterie 459 [five StuG III, three PzKpfw III]
schwere Artillerie-Abteilung 506 [four 10cm/seven 15cm]
8.Panzer-Division (General der Panzertruppen Erich Brandenberger)
    I./Panzer-Regiment 10 (25 Pz38t)
    I., II./Panzergrenadier-Regiment 8 (Oberst von Wagner)
    I., II./Panzergrenadier-Regiment 28 (Oberstleutnant Hans Freiherr von Wolff)
    Kradschützen-Bataillon 8
    Kradschützen-Bataillon 30

Jagdkommando 8
Panzerjäger-Abteilung 43
 schwere Artillerie-Abteilung 846 [15cm]
 schwere Artillerie-Abteilung 833 [21cm]
6 December 1942
1.SS-Infanterie-Brigade (mot.) (SS-Oberführer Karl Hermann)
 Frikorps Danmark
6.Luftwaffe Feld-Division (Generalleutnant Rüdiger von Heyking)
schwere Artillerie-Abteilung 845 [15cm]
Heeres-Pionier-Bataillon 743
12 December 1942
Grenadier-Regiment 504 [291.Infanterie-Division]
1.(Go)/VK(S) V [Go-242 gliders, He 111]
15 December 1942
I./Panzer-Regiment 15 (Major Heinrich Pricken) [30 PzKpfw III, three
 PzKpfw IV]
28 December 1942
Panzer-Abteilung 18
2./schwere Artillerie-Abteilung 817 [17cm]
31 December 1942
5./Luftlandegeschwader 2 [Go 242 gliders]

3 January 1943
205.Infanterie-Division (Generalleutnant Paul Seyffardt)
 I., II./Grenadier-Regiment 335
 II./Grenadier Regiment 358
331.Infanterie-Division (Generalmajor Franz Beyer)
 I., II./Grenadier-Regiment 558
 I./Grenadier-Regiment 559
Jäger-Bataillon 6
8 January 1943
205.Infanterie-Division (Generalleutnant Paul Seyffardt)
 II., III./Grenadier Regiment 353
 III./Grenadier Regiment 358
10 January 1943
331.Infanterie-Division (Generalmajor Franz Beyer)
 I., II./Grenadier-Regiment 557
 II./Grenadier-Regiment 559
 Aufklärungs-Abteilung 331
13 January 1943
III./Fallschirmjäger-Regiment 1 (7.Flieger-Division)

Air Support

General der Flieger Robert Ritter von Greim's Luftwaffenkommando Ost was responsible for providing air support to LIX.Armee-Korps. The closest units to Velikiye Luki were Generalleutnant Johannes Fink's 2.Flieger-Division formations based at Vitebsk. Fink had a total of about 107 operational aircraft in November 1942, not including transports and auxiliary aircraft. Jagdgruppe 51's pilots had scored impressive aerial victories over the 3rd Air Army during the summer of 1942, but by early November one of its *Gruppen* was transferred to Sicily, another to the Leningrad sector and another to East Prussia to re-equip with the Fw 190A fighter. The remaining *Gruppe*, IV./Jagdgeschwader 51, was heavily outnumbered by the enemy and its veteran pilots were still flying the Bf 109F-2 model. The IV./Jagdgeschwader 51 had to provide fighter cover over a wide area and typically only one *Staffeln* operated over the Velikiye Luki sector. Similarly, most of Fink's bombers had been transferred to other fronts, leaving him with a single *Gruppe* of Ju 88 bombers and one *Gruppe* of Ju 87 Stukas at the start of the Soviet winter offensive. The Luftwaffe was stretched very thinly in November 1942 and the left flank of Heeresgruppe Mitte was regarded as a low priority sector. Instead, most of von Greim's resources were devoted to supporting 9.Armee in the Rzhev salient. Prior to the Soviet offensive, Luftwaffenkommando Ost did launch some small raids against rail yards behind the 3rd Shock Army, but these efforts failed to disrupt Soviet preparations.

Once encircled, the garrison in Velikiye Luki was completely dependent upon aerial resupply, but Luftwaffenkommando Ost's transport assets were negligible. One *Gruppe* of Ju 52 transports had been based at Vitebsk, but once Operation *Uranus* began, it was transferred south to join the other six transport *Gruppen* in Russia. By late November 1942, virtually all of the Ju 52 transports in Russia were supporting 6.Armee at Stalingrad. Due to the lack of transports, Luftwaffenkommando Ost was forced to improvise an airlift with bombers and Stuka dive-bombers using supply containers (*Abwurfbehälter für Nachschub*); typically, these could only carry up to 250kg of supplies. It was not until mid-December that one *Gruppe* of the new Go 242 gliders was made available, which enabled heavier payloads to be delivered.

OPPOSING PLANS

SOVIET

On 5 November, Purkayev reported to Stavka in Moscow to receive guidance on upcoming operations for his Kalinin Front. In three weeks, the Kalinin Front was expected to attack the west side of the Rzhev salient with its 22nd, 39th and 41st armies, while the Western Front attacked the east side of the salient with its 20th Army. Operation *Mars*, conceived by General Georgy Zhukov, was intended to slice through both sides of the salient and encircle the German 9.Armee. The bulk of Purkayev's Kalinin Front would be committed to Operation *Mars*. However, Soviet intelligence had detected some of the German unit transfers related to Operation *Taubenschlag* and were probably aware that von Manstein's headquarters had relocated to Vitebsk. Stavka correctly assessed that the Germans were considering a spoiling attack from Velikiye Luki towards Toropets, which could negatively affect the Kalinin Front's role in Operation *Mars*. Consequently, Stavka ordered Purkayev to prepare a secondary operation with the 3rd Shock Army to capture Velikiye Luki and Nevel. The Velikiye Luki operation would occur concurrently with Operation *Mars* and was intended to pre-empt any German riposte. Galitski's 3rd Shock Army was reinforced between 10 and 24 November with the 5th Guards Rifle Corps and the 2nd Mechanized Corps, along with some additional artillery. Gromov's 3rd Air Army was also heavily reinforced.

According to the plan developed by Galitski's staff, the main effort would be made by the 5th Guards Rifle Corps 10–12km south of Velikiye Luki, between Kupuy and Bulynino. Soviet partisans had confirmed that this area was only lightly held by the Germans and that the 20km gap between the garrison in Velikiye Luki and Infanterie-Regiment 251 in Polibino was only held by two security battalions. Galitski expected the three veteran rifle divisions in 5th Guards Rifle Corps

Soviet airmen trudge through the snow to their Pe-2R reconnaissance aircraft. Operations by 3rd Air Army tended to be less impaired by winter weather than the Luftwaffe, even though the Soviet airmen were usually flying from primitive front-line airstrips. The 3rd Air Army had one regiment of Pe-2R reconnaissance planes. (Nik Cornish at www.Stavka.org.uk)

to smash through the thinly held German front south of Velikiye Luki, then advance west to sever the two rail lines leading to Velikiye Luki. The 381st Rifle Division would attack north of Velikiye Luki and envelop the city, then link up with 5th Guards Rifle Corps. Once the German garrison was isolated, Generalmajor Ivan P. Korchagin's 2nd Mechanized Corps would be committed to exploit the breach south of the city and push on to Novosokolniki. By capturing Novosokolniki, any hope for a German relief operation would be crushed. Another group, consisting of the 257th and 357th Rifle divisions, was tasked with destroying the encircled garrison in Velikiye Luki. Generalmajor Mikhail M. Gromov's 3rd Air Army was tasked with providing air support, particularly interfering with any German aerial resupply operations. In Stavka's view, successful offensives against the Rzhev salient and Velikiye Luki would shatter Heeresgruppe Mitte's left flank and cause the remnants to fall back in headlong retreat.

A Soviet 152mm ML-20 howitzer is moved to the front by artillery tractor. Note that the crew are walking on foot behind the tractor. The Kalinin Front operated in a region that had few roads, which made it difficult to move heavy artillery and supplies, particularly during winter. (Nik Cornish at www.Stavka.org.uk)

Galitsky's plan had the advantage of simplicity, concentration of force and clear objectives, but the 3rd Shock Army lacked any appreciable reserves and some of the forces provided were on short-term loan. In particular, Purkayev wanted the Guards units released as soon as possible to support other operations. Korchagin's 2nd Mechanized Corps was expected to double as both an exploitation force and a mobile reserve in case the Germans mounted a relief operation. It is also interesting that Galitski apparently made little provision for coordinating his offensive with local partisans for either intelligence gathering or attacks on German lines of communication. Purkayev expected the Velikiye Luki operation to be completed in about a week, but there was no plan to follow up success with an immediate push towards Vitebsk. The logistical support for Galitski's 3rd Shock Army was also tailored to a short-term, limited-objective attack. In large part, the lack of a follow-on plan was a recognition that the front had attempted too many simultaneous

A column of Soviet T-70 light tanks advances towards the front. In order to conduct the encirclement of Velikiye Luki, the 3rd Shock Army was provided with the 2nd Mechanized Corps, which the Germans did not expect. However, the corps was not employed as a single formation, but instead split up into brigades for infantry support. (Nik Cornish at www. Stavka.org.uk)

operations in the first winter counter-offensive and was not going to repeat that error. Once Velikiye Luki had fallen and Gruppe Chevallerie had been defeated, Purkayev could devote all of the Kalinin Front's resources towards sustaining the attack against the Rzhev salient. General Zhukov visited Galitski's headquarters on 19 November to review the planning, and supposedly told him: 'It doesn't matter whether you take Novosokolniki or not – we will still consider the task accomplished if you attract the enemy's forces and he cannot remove them from your sector for transfer to the south.'

In preparation for the offensive, the Soviets began interdicting German supply lines, harassing supply convoys with artillery, mines and air attacks in mid-November. Unlike the Western Allies, the Soviet Air Force rarely flew more than 30km behind the front on interdiction missions. One exception was an attack by 45 bombers on Vitebsk in late October, which temporarily disrupted German communications. However, most of 3rd Air Army's interdiction efforts consisted of small raids by Il-2 Sturmoviks on nearby targets, such as the train stations in Nevel and Velikiye Luki, which inflicted minimal damage. On 11 November, 30 bombers from 3rd Air Army conducted a larger raid on Velikiye Luki's train station, but inflicted only minimal damage. About two weeks before the offensive, the 3rd Shock Army began aggressive, company-size reconnaissance actions along the Lovat River, which caused 83.Infanterie-Division to reinforce some of its combat outposts. However, effective use of *maskirovka* (deception) tactics prevented Gruppe Chevallerie from detecting the arrival of a complete Guards rifle corps along the Lovat south of Velikiye Luki.

German infantry on the forward edge of the battle area – apparently a patrol preparing to move forward. Note the bunker on the left. At the beginning of the Soviet offensive, Gruppe Meyer was occupying temporary fieldworks and had not established strong defensive positions. Indeed, two-thirds of 83.Infanterie-Division was essentially deployed in small combat outposts. (Nik Cornish at www.Stavka.org.uk)

GERMAN

With German forces stretched thin on the Eastern Front by mid-1942, it was questionable whether exposed positions like Demyansk, Velikiye Luki and Rzhev were worth the cost in resources of holding. Many senior German officers preferred the 'Elastic Defence' doctrine, of ceding some terrain in order to preserve valuable units and mount powerful counter-attacks once the enemy was off-balance. However, Hitler did not relish the idea of relinquishing terrain even briefly, and on 8 September, he issued a Führer order which specified that commanders could not conduct tactical withdrawals without his permission. Consequently, Hitler's order undermined German defensive planning by an insistence upon positional, rather than flexible, defences. Both von Kluge and von der Chevallerie would have preferred abandoning Velikiye Luki in order to create a strong front on the line Novosokolniki–Nevel, but Hitler would not agree to relinquish even this useless stretch of frozen marshland.

Nevertheless, Gruppe Chevallerie considered itself prepared for a protracted siege battle at Velikiye Luki. Over the course of the summer,

A German 8.8cm Flak gun is moved into position by an SdKfz 11 half-track. Note the numerous 'kill' markings on the 8.8cm gun. The Luftwaffe contributed a few 88cm Flak guns to provide direct support to the army, which helped to stiffen the defence of key positions. (Nik Cornish at www.Stavka.org.uk)

Infanterie-Regiment 277 had completed a 360-degree ring of fortifications around the city, which were divided into three defensive sectors: north-east, south and west. The garrison had its own artillery support and had enough food and ammunition to hold out for at least two weeks. However, Generalmajor Theodor Scherer was not so confident when he took command of 83.Infanterie-Division on 7 November. He was surprised to find that the defences on the west side of Velikiye Luki were relatively weak and that the garrison was expected to hold 22km of field works with just 7,000 personnel, only one-third of whom were combat troops. Some minefields had been laid around the city approaches, but Gruppe Chevallerie focused the main minelaying effort at Velizh, not Velikiye Luki. The 83.Infanterie-Division was provided only 2,000 anti-tank T-minen and 1,500 anti-personnel S-minen to emplace across its entire front, which meant the German obstacle belt was thin. It was also evident that the garrison was really only prepared for a short siege, since the artillery units in Velikiye Luki had enough ammunition for about ten days of combat. Nor had any efforts been made to establish an airstrip in Velikiye Luki in case Luftwaffe aerial resupply or casualty evacuation was required. Scherer's experience in the 105-day siege of Kholm had taught him that prior preparations were more useful than ad hoc combat improvisations. As a first step, he ordered Oberstleutnant von Sass to improve the defences on the west side of Velikiye Luki. Looking at his dispersed division, Scherer recognized that not only was Velikiye Luki vulnerable to encirclement, but the entire 83.Infanterie-Division was also at risk in the event of a major Soviet attack. None of his three regiments were within supporting range of each other, and he was forced to plug the gaps between his regiments with security units. Once von Manstein's forces began to leave, Scherer recognized that 83.Infanterie-Division would be virtually on its own.

A German soldier with an MG 34 machine gun watches to his front, past a row of barbed-wire obstacles. Note that visibility into the adjacent wooded area is limited to a short distance. The outer defences of Velikiye Luki included some positions like this, to keep Red Army patrols from getting close enough to spot the main defensive positions. (Nik Cornish at www.Stavka.org.uk)

Despite the strong hedgehog position built in Velikiye Luki, the area north of the city was protected by just a few isolated strongpoints. While the marshland and forests north of Velikiye Luki were a barrier to larger units, Scherer had little doubt that Soviet ski troops could move through this region to envelop the city from the north. The direct route to Novosokolniki – 21km to the west – was also guarded by a few security detachments. Likewise, the Nevel–Velikiye Luki rail link was too tenuous to survive a major enemy attack. Scherer believed that Velikiye Luki would likely be surrounded in the event of a major enemy offensive and that Gruppe Chevallerie would have difficulty mounting a timely rescue operation with its own resources. Having weathered the earlier crisis at Velizh, von der Chevallerie was confident that a relief operation could be mounted from Novosokolniki before the garrison in Velikiye Luki was overwhelmed.

The basic tactical plan for the defence of Velikiye Luki was simple: fight tooth and nail for each strongpoint, then fall back to the next prepared position, forcing the Soviets into a bloody battle of attrition. German artillery in Velikiye Luki was expected to crush Soviet infantry assaults. During the first winter battles, the Soviets had demonstrated great difficulty in assaulting fortified positions and the use of crude mob tactics had led to crippling losses. The Citadel, on the western side of the city, was surrounded on three sides by the Lovat River and its thick earth-and-mortar walls were nearly impervious to artillery fire; this was judged to be the final fallback position, if necessary. However, German defensive planning was undermined by their misjudgement about the ability of the Soviets to learn from their previous mistakes and to improve their tactical capabilities. If the Soviets employed heavy artillery and improved infantry tactics, an encircled garrison could not win a battle of attrition.

The most significant problem with von der Chevallerie's optimistic defensive plans was the availability of reserves to conduct a relief operation. Once the forces earmarked for *Taubenschlag* began to depart, Gruppe Chevallerie was left with no significant tactical reserves. Based upon Generalfeldmarschall Günther von Kluge's decision, virtually all of Heeresgruppe Mitte's reserves were committed to reinforce 9.Armee in the Rzhev salient, leaving nothing for Gruppe Chevallerie. Consequently, von der Chevallerie would have to beg for reinforcements to mount what should have been a simple division-size relief operation. Nor did Generalfeldmarschall Georg Wilhelm von Küchler's neighbouring Heeresgruppe Nord have much in the way of tactical reserves, since eight full divisions from 16.Armee were still tied down defending the vulnerable Demyansk salient, and Kholm also required a large force to hold. Due to the retention of Demyansk and Kholm, Küchler had no reserves left to protect the boundary with Heeresgruppe Mitte. Instead of taking responsibility for defence of the inter-army group boundary that ran through the Velikiye Luki sector, both von Kluge and von Küchler left it up to von der Chevallerie to muddle through with wholly inadequate resources.

A German artillery forward observer surveys the front line from inside the upper floor of a building. The Germans had positioned a special artillery observation detachment in Velikiye Luki for the specific purpose of directing long-range artillery fires against the enemy. Initially, these observers played a major role in repulsing the first Soviet attacks on the city, but eventually they were committed as infantrymen, as was the rest of the garrison. (Nik Cornish at www. Stavka.org.uk)

The 3rd Shock Army offensive begins, 24–29 November 1942

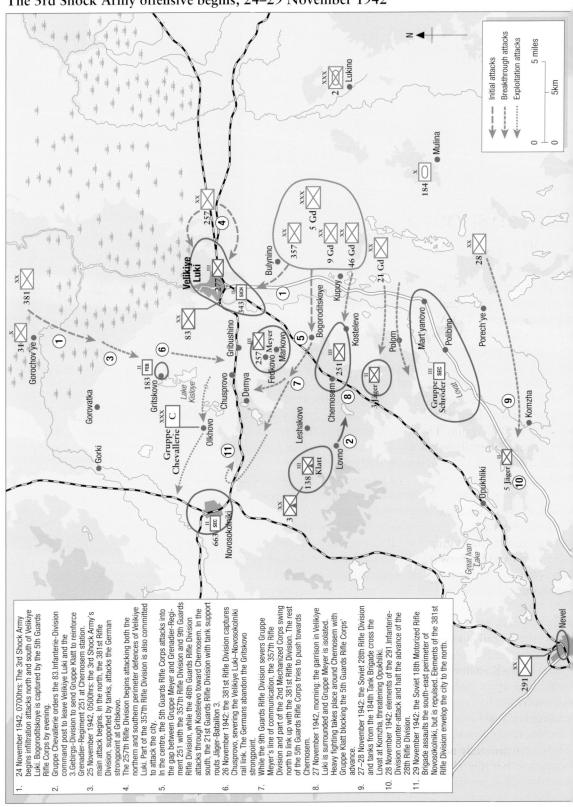

1. 24 November 1942, 0700hrs: The 3rd Shock Army begins infiltration attacks north and south of Velikiye Luki. Bogoroditskoye is captured by the 5th Guards Rifle Corps by evening.
2. Gruppe Chevallerie orders the 83.Infanterie-Division command post to leave Velikiye Luki and the 3.Gebirgs-Division to send Gruppe Klatt to reinforce Grenadier-Regiment 251 at Chernosem station.
3. 25 November 1942, 0500hrs: the 3rd Shock Army's main attack begins. In the north, the 381st Rifle Division, supported by tanks, attacks the German strongpoint at Gritskovo.
4. The 257th Rifle Division begins attacking both the northern and southern perimeter defences of Velikiye Luki. Part of the 357th Rifle Division is also committed to attack the city.
5. In the centre, the 5th Guards Rifle Corps attacks into the gap between Gruppe Meyer and Grenadier-Regiment 251 with the 357th Rifle Division and 9th Guards Rifle Division, while the 46th Guards Rifle Division attacks through Kostelevo toward Chernosem. In the south, the 21st Guards Rifle Division with tank support routs Jäger-Bataillon 3.
6. 26 November 1942: the 381st Rifle Division captures Chusprovo, severing the Velikiye Luki–Novosokolniki rail link. The Germans abandon the Gritskovo strongpoint.
7. While the 9th Guards Rifle Division severs Gruppe Meyer's line of communication, the 357th Rifle Division and part of the 2nd Mechanized Corps swing north to link up with the 381st Rifle Division. The rest of the 5th Guards Rifle Corps tries to push towards Chernosem.
8. 27 November 1942, morning: the garrison in Velikiye Luki is surrounded and Gruppe Meyer is isolated. Heavy fighting takes place around Chernosem with Gruppe Klatt blocking the 5th Guards Rifle Corps' advance.
9. 27–28 November 1942: the Soviet 28th Rifle Division and tanks from the 184th Tank Brigade cross the Lovat at Komzha, threatening Opukhliki.
10. 28 November 1942: elements of the 291.Infanterie-Division counter-attack and halt the advance of the 28th Rifle Division.
11. 29 November 1942: the Soviet 18th Motorized Rifle Brigade assaults the south-east perimeter of Novosokolniki, but is repulsed. Elements of the 381st Rifle Division envelop the city to the north.

34

THE CAMPAIGN

THE 3RD SHOCK ARMY OFFENSIVE BEGINS, 24–30 NOVEMBER 1942

For a variety of reasons, Gruppe Chevallerie failed to detect that the 3rd Shock Army was about to launch a major offensive. Soviet *maskirovka* efforts helped to conceal the arrival of Beloborodov's 5th Guards Rifle Corps and Korchagin's 2nd Mechanized Corps in the Velikiye Luki sector. The four rifle divisions in the Central Attack Group assembled east of the Lovat River, then began quietly infiltrating across the river several days before the start of the offensive. Likewise, the one rifle division and one rifle brigade of the Northern Attack Group assembled in marshy, wooded terrain about 10km north of Velikiye Luki. Prior to the beginning of the offensive, there was a no-man's-land about 2km wide along the Lovat and about 4km wide around Velikiye Luki. There were some skirmishes with German patrols, but Gruppe Chevallerie did not see a pattern. Most of the Soviet heavy artillery and tanks were kept back and only moved into forward assembly areas late on 23 November, which helped to deceive the Germans. Fog along the Lovat also helped to mask Soviet movements.

Just prior to the beginning of the Soviet offensive, Scherer moved his forward division command post into Velikiye Luki and von der Chevallerie had his group headquarters established in Olkhovo, 8km east of Novosokolniki. Gruppe Meyer was located 9km south-west of Velikiye Luki, just west of the rail line and Oberstleutnant Johann Giehl's Grenadier-Regiment 251 was defending the Chernosem–Kostelevo sector. Due to Hitler's rigid insistence upon holding Velikiye Luki, virtually the entire 83.Infanterie-Division was deployed to protect the Nevel–Velikiye Luki rail line, although there was no continuous front and the German units were generally not within supporting distance of each other. On the night of 23/24 November, the Germans began to pick up indications that something was afoot. The forward positions of

Soviet sappers cut through German barbed-wire obstacles in order to open the way for assault infantry groups. Note that this is occurring in broad daylight; normally, this kind of battlefield preparation would occur under the cover of darkness – indicating that this may be training prior to the beginning of the Soviet offensive. (Courtesy of the Central Museum of the Armed Forces, Moscow via Stavka)

Grenadier-Regiment 251 and Grenadier-Regiment 257 were probed by company-size elements and hit with 122mm and 152mm artillery ranging fire; by chance, the Germans captured a prisoner who revealed that he was from the 46th Guards Rifle Division – a formation not previously seen in this sector. The German garrison in Velikiye Luki was also lightly probed, and during the night, German outposts heard mines detonating on their southern perimeter. The 3rd Shock Army also lobbed 41 152mm rounds into the city, another sign that there was more enemy artillery in the region than previously thought. Although Galitski was trying to avoid tipping his hand too soon, it was also necessary to gauge the enemy defences prior to the main assault. Despite alerting the Germans to some extent, the Soviet reconnaissance activity succeeded in identifying a large gap between Gruppe Meyer and Giehl's Grenadier-Regiment 251 – this is where the main effort would be made.

Unlike other Soviet offensives, the Velikiye Luki operation (*Velikolukskaya operatsiya*) did not begin with a lengthy artillery preparation and a single jump-off time. Rather, the operation began as a staggered infiltration attack with units assigned objectives by 3rd Shock Army but attacking at different times; secondary sources which suggest that the attacks began all at one specific time are incorrect. When the sun rose on the morning of 24 November 1942, at 0648hrs, units simply began advancing towards their objectives, and attacks escalated throughout the day. Heavy morning fog covered the frozen landscape and did not lift until 1000hrs. The temperature was around -3° C (26° F). Beloborodov's artillery commander, Polkovnik Vasily V. Tsarkov, had advised that since Soviet observers could not observe the German main line of resistance (*Hauptkampflinie* – HKL) west of the Lovat, an artillery preparation would be ineffective. Instead, Tsarkov's artillery only conducted harassing fire on suspected German outposts. As per doctrine, the Germans had deployed platoon-size combat outposts 3–4km forward of their HKL, to provide early warning of an attack.

Each Soviet rifle division advanced in two echelons, with one regiment in the first and two regiments in the second. The Soviet infantry, most wearing white camouflage suits, advanced cautiously towards the German outpost line. Some dragged machine guns on skis or boxes of extra ammunition and grenades. The first major attack was launched by General-major Sergei I. Karapetian's 46th Guards Rifle Division against Hauptmann Friedholm Günther's II./Grenadier-Regiment 251 near Kostelevo around 0900hrs. At least two Soviet rifle battalions, supported by heavy artillery and multiple rocket-launchers, were committed in the initial assault. Two German outposts outside the town were overrun and by 1300hrs, Karapetian committed more of his infantry and a few light tanks. Hauptmann Günther was badly wounded by a direct artillery strike on his command post and his battalion suffered over 100 casualties, but the Germans managed to hold onto Kostelevo for the time being. Karapetian manoeuvred one of his other regiments, the 508th Rifle Regiment, into a gap in the German line south of Kostelevo and this unit advanced 2km. Further south, General-major Denis V. Mikhailov's 21st Guards Rifle Division attacked Gruppe Schröder and overran one of its combat outposts.

The main attack by Beloborodov's 5th Guards Rifle Corps began to develop in the late afternoon. The tanks that were supposed to support the 5th Guards Rifle Corps's attack were late to arrive and move forward,

A group of German prisoners captured during the early stages of the Soviet winter counter-offensive. Note that the prisoners are clean-shaven and not particularly dirty, suggesting that they may have been support troops. Small numbers of German troops were scooped up by the initial Soviet attacks, but there was no large haul of prisoners during the campaign. (Nik Cornish at www.Stavka.org.uk)

which delayed the attack. General-major Ignatiy V. Prostiakov's 9th Guards Rifle Division encountered heavy resistance from a German combat outpost in the village of Bogoroditskoye around 1400hrs and could not capture this position until a Soviet tank platoon arrived around 1800hrs. Kapitan Nikolay S. Galpin led his 2nd Battalion, 18th Guards Rifle Regiment in a night attack which finally overwhelmed the outpost – the main success for 5th Guards Rifle Corps on the first day. Beloborodov intended to use the village as a launching pad to advance into the gap between Gruppe Meyer and Giehl's Grenadier-Regiment 251. The III./Grenadier-Regiment 251's outer perimeter was hit hard around 1700hrs by enemy infantry with tank and artillery support; one outpost was wiped out, but the remainder of the battalion held firm and repulsed the enemy attack. Three kilometres to the north-east, Gruppe Meyer's main strongpoint on the rail line was Stützpunkt Münsingen on Hill 152.1, held by a single company. The 9th Guards Rifle Division began its assault on Stützpunkt Münsingen with the 22nd Guards Rifle Regiment at dusk, but was repulsed. Soviet casualties were substantial and the Germans took 30 prisoners. However, during the night, Soviet infantry began advancing west of the rail line, severing the link to Gruppe Meyer and Velikiye Luki. Winter nights were long in this region, typically lasting 14 hours.

By late afternoon, von der Chevallerie estimated that he was being attacked by two previously unidentified Soviet rifle divisions, but enemy intentions were still unclear. Nevertheless, von der Chevallerie appealed for reinforcements. Although von Manstein and most of his staff had already departed the area, 11.Armee's chief of staff – Generalmajor Friedrich Schulz – was still in Vitebsk to supervise the rail movement of the army's formations, and around 2000hrs, he agreed to release one regiment from 3.Gebirgs-Division and one from 291.Infanterie-Division, along with Sturmgeschütz-Abteilung 185, to Gruppe Chevallerie to deal with the enemy offensive. Gruppe Klatt (Gebirgsjäger-Regiment 138 and one artillery battalion) were located in Senkina-Gora, 8km west of Chernosem station; Klatt was ordered to immediately move to support Giehl's hard-pressed Grenadier-Regiment 251. Grenadier-Regiment 505 (from 291.Infanterie-Division) had already left Nevel bound for Smolensk, but it was turned around and ordered to move to reinforce Gruppe Schröder.

It started to snow during the night of 24/25 November and the slippery roads hindered the German tactical movements. Mikhailov's 21st Guards Rifle Division attacked Gruppe Schröder with the 59th Guards Rifle Regiment before dawn, and after heavy fighting, captured Stolpino. Mikhailov was more successful south of Kostelevo, where one infantry regiment with tank support managed to inflict some damage on Jäger-Battalion 3 and then attacked two German 10.5cm howitzer batteries near Jeshewizy around 1500hrs. The German artillerymen managed to knock out three Soviet tanks at point-blank range, but one battery commander was killed. However, before Mikhailov could exploit this success, one battalion (III./Gebirgsjäger-Regiment 138) from Gruppe Klatt arrived, which managed to halt the Soviet advance. Klatt's other battalion was sent to support the hard-pressed II./Grenadier-Regiment 251 at Kostelevo, which enabled it to repulse further attacks by the 46th Guards Rifle Division. Klatt's Gebirgsjäger were reinforced with a battery of assault guns. Although the arrival of Gruppe Klatt helped the Germans to hold onto Chernosem station, it was clear that the Soviets had cut the rail line to Velikiye Luki and that the connection with Gruppe Meyer was in danger. Giehl had already moved the III./Grenadier-Regiment 251 north along the rail line to Meyer, but soon found itself cut off as well. Prostiakov's 9th Guards Rifle Division had managed to encircle two German company-size outposts, and by dusk, had advanced 3km west of the rail line. Gruppe Meyer was able to repulse multiple attacks by 9th Guards Rifle Division and claimed to have destroyed 11 tanks, but was now nearly isolated and running short of ammunition.

Further north, Polkovnik Boris S. Maslov's 381st Rifle Division and Podpolkovnik A. V. Yakushev's 31st Rifle Brigade advanced out of the marshland north of Velikiye Luki to sever the Novosokolniki–Velikiye Luki rail line. Around 0500hrs, Yakushev's brigade and about ten light tanks attacked the German strongpoint at Gritskovo. The Germans had fortified several villages west of Velikiye Luki to protect the road and rail connections to Novosokolniki, but they had not come under serious attack before and Gritskovo was held by a company from the divisional field replacement battalion (Feld Ersatz-Bataillon). When von Sass heard about Soviet tanks at Gritskovo, he dispatched a Panzerjäger detachment to provide support. Although the Panzerjägers enabled the Gritskovo strongpoint to hold out, Maslov sent his 1261st Rifle Regiment to sever the road and rail links to Novosokolniki, while his other two rifle regiments advanced west towards Novosokolniki. The only unit in this area was the Sicherungs-Bataillon 343, with detachments scattered along the roads and rail line. Polkovnik Aleksandr L. Kronik's 357th Rifle Division also began probing the outer German defences at Velikiye Luki, but no major attacks were launched yet.

During the night of 25/26 November, the 3rd Shock Army continued to attack – sustained night fighting was highly unusual on the Eastern Front – and German casualties were mounting. Von der Chevallerie appealed to Heeresgruppe Mitte for additional reinforcements, but the Soviet offensive

A German machine-gun team waits in a frozen streambed. Once surrounded, Gruppe Meyer quickly established a 360-degree defence around several key villages, and thanks to its attached firepower support assets, it was able to repulse most Soviet attacks. Note that the German troops are well equipped with winter kit, including gloves, balaclavas and winter camouflage jackets – a far cry from the first winter in Russia. (Nik Cornish at www. Stavka.org.uk)

against the Rzhev salient had just begun and von Kluge committed virtually all of his armour – totalling seven *Panzer-Divisionen* – to support 9.Armee, leaving virtually nothing to deal with a crisis in the Velikiye Luki sector. Gruppe Chevallerie was forced to turn to OKH, which ordered Heeresgruppe Nord to release some forces to deal with the 3rd Shock Army's offensive. Von Küchler provided 8.Panzer-Division and the 20.Infanterie-Division (mot.), neither of which had much offensive capability. The 8.Panzer-Division, located 70km north of Velikiye Luki, had just 25 obsolete Czech-made Pz. 38(t) tanks and its infantry units had been reduced to 45 per cent of their authorized strength – totalling five battalions with 2,407 men. The 20.Infanterie-Division (mot.) was in better shape, with six infantry battalions and a *Kradschützen-Bataillon* (motorcycle battalion), but was located near Novgorod and would take a couple of days to reach the Velikiye Luki sector by rail. The OKH also agreed to return another regiment from 291.Infanterie-Division and assign it to Gruppe Chevallerie, but von Kluge managed to keep one of its regiments. In the interim, Gruppe Chevallerie had to hold until reinforcements arrived.

On the morning of 26 November, Prostiakov's 9th Guards Rifle Division launched regimental-size attacks, supported by artillery and tanks, which eventually forced Gruppe Meyer to abandon Stützpunkt Münsingen. Meyer was pushed back into a hedgehog position around the villages of Teleshnikovo and Markova. Meanwhile, other Soviet troops pushed past Gruppe Meyer's open flank and moved north towards Maslov's 381st Rifle Division. Kronik's 357th Rifle Division, which thus far had only played a minor role in the offensive, advanced to occupy the bridge over the Lovat south-west of Velikiye Luki. Kronik also launched a battalion-size attack against the Felt Factory on the southern edge of the city, but was repulsed with over 100 casualties. Nevertheless, von Sass ordered the Feld Ersatz-Bataillon company to abandon the Gritskovo strongpoint and withdraw into Velikiye Luki,

A German Gebirgsjäger near Velikiye Luki, January 1943. The mountain infantrymen of Klatt's Gebirgsjäger-Regiment 138 were the most solid unit employed during the Velikiye Luki campaign, but this unit suffered crippling casualties. (Süddeutsche Zeitung Bild 00003137, Foto: Scherl)

which made it easier for Maslov's 381st Rifle Division to push south to link up with 9th Guards Rifle Division and 357th Rifle Division. Soviet troops from the 1261st Rifle Regiment occupied Chusprovo, on the Novosokolniki–Velikiye Luki rail line, and the two remaining German-held strongpoints (Ostriany and Velebetskoe) on the rail line were in danger of being surrounded. By dusk, Maslov's scouts had already appeared near Gruppe Chevallerie's command post at Olkhovo.

In the south, Beloborodov was frustrated by the slow progress of his 5th Guards Rifle Corps, particularly the inability of the 46th Guards Rifle Division to capture Kostelevo. Gruppe Klatt, supported by nine assault guns, was able to counter-attack and recover some ground, as well as knocking out a number of enemy tanks. However, continuous Soviet attacks had severely reduced II./Grenadier-Regiment 251, and Kostelevo was no longer worth the price in blood. Elements of 9th Guards Rifle Division had already begun to outflank the position in Chernosem, and Giehl pulled back his battered battalion to hold the critical rail station. Further south, Mikhailov's 21st Guards Rifle Division continued to put heavy pressure on Gruppe Schröder, and Jäger-Bataillon 3 was forced to retreat. Polkovnik Sergei A. Kniazkov's 28th Rifle Division and the 184th Tank Brigade attacked the right flank of Gruppe Schröder and threatened to isolate it. Kniazkov also managed to capture a crossing over the Lovat at Komzha, which threatened the German supply base at Opukhliki.

By midday on 26 November, von der Chevallerie had to decide where and when to commit the incoming reinforcements, given the information available. Since the garrison in Velikiye Luki was not hard-pressed, he assessed that the most urgent tasks appeared to be to reinforce the crumbling right flank and restore the rail link to Gruppe Meyer. Generalmajor Erich Jaschke, who was leading the advance Kampfgruppe from his 20.Infanterie-Division (mot.), was ordered to detrain in Nevel and move north-east to support Gruppe Schröder with the bulk of his forces. Gruppe Jaschke would initially consist of two battalions from 20.Infanterie-Division (mot.) and two battalions from Grenadier-Regiment 505, plus Jäger-Bataillon 1. A smaller Kampfgruppe, Gruppe Häheler, with two infantry battalions and a few tanks, would advance directly along the rail line to link up with Gruppe Klatt. Von der Chevallerie's decision was rather cautious and failed to mass decisive combat power in either sector. It was also highly questionable why the largest effort was being made to support Gruppe Schröder when the bulk of Scherer's 83.Infanterie-Division was already surrounded and threatened with annihilation. Von der Chevallerie decided that General Erich Brandenberger's 8.Panzer-Division, which was assembling at Nasva station 25km north of Novosokolniki, would clear up the enemy infiltration west of Velikiye Luki on its own.

Although the German reaction to the surprise Soviet offensive was fast, it was not fast enough. By noon on 27 November, elements of the 381st Rifle Division and 357th Rifle Division linked up west of Velikiye Luki, completing the encirclement of the city. At this point, the German garrison in Velikiye Luki numbered approximately 6,875 personnel, including about 1,850 from von Sass' Grenadier-Regiment 277, 500 personnel from Sicherungs-Bataillon 336 and about 800 artillerymen. Maslov's 381st Rifle Division also succeeded in forcing Gruppe Chevallerie to abandon its command post in Olkhovo and retreat to Novosokolniki. Scherer tried to send Panzerzug 7 along the rail line to reach the Velebetskoe strongpoint 5km west of Velikiye Luki, but found the line blocked by Soviet troops. Now Scherer was ordered to organize the defence of Novosokolniki. Even before the encirclement of Velikiye Luki was complete, the 257th Rifle Division and 357th Rifle Division began to launch strong attacks upon the southern perimeter of the city, but German artillery fire broke up the attacks. The 357th Rifle Division did succeed in isolating the German garrisons in the Felt Factory and Bayreuth strongpoints, but no positions were taken. Von der Chevallerie asked von Greim's Luftwaffenkommando Ost to begin aerial resupply operations for the encircled garrison in Velikiye Luki and Gruppe Meyer, but virtually all transports had been sent south to join the Stalingrad airlift operation. In fact, von Sass would not receive his first aerial resupply for another ten days. Poor weather, including sleet and frequent snowstorms, made it difficult for the Luftwaffe to identify and attack enemy troop concentrations. In contrast, 3rd Air Army was regularly bombing and strafing German positions.

On the night of 27/28 November, Soviet scouts from 9th Guards Rifle Division captured some German prisoners, who revealed the commitment of Gruppe Klatt and an impending German relief operation. Alerted by this information, Galitski decided to commit the 18th Mechanized Brigade from 2nd Mechanized Corps to try and capture Novosokolniki before German reinforcements could arrive. Maslov's 381st Rifle Division was already closing in on the north-eastern outskirts of the city with the 1259th and 1261st Rifle regiments. Although the Germans had 5,000 troops in Novosokolniki, very few combat troops were in the city; aside from a 500-man security battalion and some Luftwaffe Flak troops, most of the personnel were either support troops from 3.Gebirgs-Division or corps-level support troops. Fieldworks had been built around the city in the summer of 1942, but there were not enough troops to man them all. Scherer rushed to organize anti-tank defences and establish a tactical radio command net to control this ad hoc collection of troops. Podpolkovnik Sergey V. Lebedev's 18th Mechanized Brigade moved through the gap between Gruppe Meyer and Grenadier-Regiment 251 during the night of 27/28 November, but did not reach the south-east

A Soviet sapper equipped with a ROKS-2 flame-thrower, which came in quite handy for neutralizing enemy bunkers in urban combat. However, these man-portable flame-throwers had a very short range and did not carry much fuel, and there were usually no more than two per infantry regiment. (Courtesy of the Central Museum of the Armed Forces, Moscow via Stavka)

INITIAL SOVIET ATTACKS ON VELIKIYE LUKI, 25–30 NOVEMBER 1942

The Soviet 3rd Shock Army completed the encirclement of Velikiye Luki on 27 November 1942, but did not make any major attacks against the city for two weeks. Instead, the 257th Rifle Division and 357th Rifle Division slowly tightened the noose, making company- and battalion-size attacks to probe the defences, and forcing the German garrison to expend ammunition.

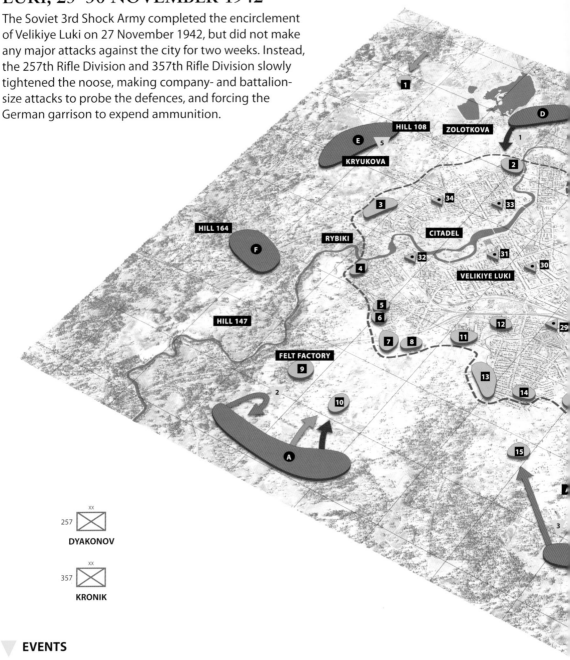

257 DYAKONOV

357 KRONIK

EVENTS

1. 25 November 1942: Soviet probing attacks begin against *Stützpunkte* Bayreuth, Hamburg and Klausenberg.

2. 26 November 1942: After an air raid on Velikiye Luki, the Soviets attack the Felt Factory and Stützpunkt Nordlingen, but the attacks are repulsed.

3. 27–28 November 1942: The Soviets use artillery, infantry and tanks to attack *Stützpunkte* Bayreuth, Tannendorf and Wesel.

4. 29 November 1942: Attacks along the perimeter increase, with more artillery support.

5. 1 December 1942: German Stukas bomb Soviet artillery positions around Velikiye Luki.

Note: gridlines are shown at intervals of 1km (0.62 miles)

KEY

→ 25 November
→ 26 November
→ 27–28 November

SOVIET:
A. 943rd Rifle Regiment (257th Rifle Division)
B. 948th Rifle Regiment (257th Rifle Division)
C. 953rd Rifle Regiment (257th Rifle Division)
D. 1188th Rifle Regiment (357th Rifle Division)
E. 1190th Rifle Regiment (357th Rifle Division)
F. 1192nd Rifle Regiment (357th Rifle Division)

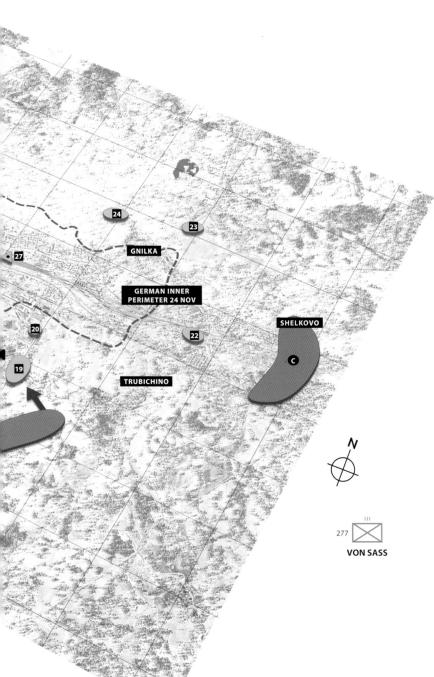

GNILKA

GERMAN INNER PERIMETER 24 NOV

SHELKOVO

TRUBICHINO

277 VON SASS

GERMAN UNITS/POSITIONS:
1. Stützpunkt Wesel
2. Stützpunkt Hamburg
3. Stützpunkt Feldberg
4. Stützpunkt Augsburg
5. Stützpunkt Innsbruck
6. Stützpunkt Würzburg
7. Stützpunkt Nürnberg
8. Stützpunkt München
9. Felt Factory
10. Stützpunkt Bayreuth
11. Stützpunkt Regensburg
12. Stützpunkt Salzburg
13. Stützpunkt Brünn
14. Stützpunkt Nordlingen
15. Stützpunkt Nordlingen Vorst
16. Stützpunkt Wien
17. Stützpunkt Tannendorf
18. Stützpunkt Preuss Berlin
19. Stützpunkt Klausenberg
20. Stützpunkt Weisses Haus
21. Stützpunkt Budapest
22. Stützpunkt Bromberg
23. Stützpunkt Brandenberg
24. Stützpunkt Braunschweig
25. Stützpunkt Falkenauge
26. Stützpunkt Kolberg
27. Nebelwerfer battery (15cm)
28. Howitzer battery (10.5cm)
29. Nebelwerfer battery (15cm and 28cm/32cm)
30. Mixed howitzer battery (10cm and 15cm)
31. Howitzer battery (10.5cm)
32. Howitzer battery (10.5cm)
33. Mixed howitzer battery (10cm and 15cm)
34. Howitzer battery (10.5cm)

A Soviet crew prepares to fire a 76.2mm regimental gun M1927. Each Soviet rifle regiment was authorized a company with four of these weapons, which were intended to provide direct support to the infantry with high-explosive and fragmentation rounds. The M1927 was small enough so that it could be used in the front line, and was useful for suppressing enemy-held buildings. (Nik Cornish at www. Stavka.org.uk)

outskirts of Novosokolniki until dusk on 28 November. Lebedev's advance guard was stopped by anti-tank guns Scherer had deployed, which persuaded the Russians not to mount a night attack.

Once Soviet armour reached the outskirts of Novosokolniki, both von Kluge and von der Chevallerie realized that the Soviet offensive was larger than they had anticipated and that the garrison in Velikiye Luki was in serious jeopardy. Von der Chevallerie relocated his corps command post to Opukhliki – apparently not wishing to risk possible encirclement in Novosokolniki. Von Kluge sent a request to OKH that the garrison in Velikiye Luki should be authorized to mount a breakout before the 3rd Shock Army fully invested the city. By abandoning the city, Gruppe Chevallerie would have a better chance to hold the line Nevel–Novosokolniki and prevent the loss of valuable combat units. However, upon learning of the request, Hitler dismissed it out of hand. He said if Kholm could hold out for 105 days, then surely Velikiye Luki could hold on until a relief operation arrived. In accordance with his defensive order, Hitler demanded that Velikiye Luki would be held at all costs. However, in contrast to the similar situation facing the encircled 6.Armee at Stalingrad, Reichsmarschall Hermann Göring made no promise to supply Velikiye Luki by air and no major ground forces were allocated for a relief operation. Instead, von der Chevallerie was expected to clear up the situation with the resources he had.

On 28 November, a period of cold, rainy weather began, which further slowed the German build-up and prevented the Luftwaffe from lending any significant support. Gruppe Jaschke had sufficient forces on hand to prevent Kniazkov's 28th Rifle Division from advancing towards Opukhliki, but was not yet capable of mounting a serious attack. Kniazkov continued to pound Gruppe Schröder, but after four days of combat, the 184th Tank Brigade had suffered crippling losses, with only 11 of its 46 tanks still operational (eight Lee, three T-60). Meanwhile, the encircled Gruppe Meyer was under continuous attack, but managed to get in some blows of its own. Meyer launched an effort to re-establish a link with Giehl's forces, led by seven assault guns. The German troops attacked the village of Botovo, which was held by lements of the 31st Guards Rifle Regiment (9th Guards Rifle Division). By chance, the regimental commander – Polkovnik Nikolai G. Dokuchaev – was n Botovo and he was killed in the action, although Meyer's troops failed o capture the village. The loss of Dokuchaev, a highly experienced combat fficer who had once served in the Tsar's elite Preobrazhensky (Life Guard) egiment, was a setback for 5th Guards Rifle Corps. Meanwhile, Gruppe Klatt was too occupied with fending off Soviet attacks around Chernosem o lend any help to Gruppe Meyer.

Brandenberger's 8.Panzer-Division was also deploying north of Novosokolniki to mount an attack into the flank of Maslov's 381st Rifle Division. Soviet partisans spotted these German movements and alerted 3rd Shock Army, which deployed Yakushev's 31st Rifle Brigade to establish defence near Ivanovo. At 0800hrs on the morning of 29 November, Brandenberger's 8.Panzer-Division attacked with five battalions on line und managed to advance about 2km before running into stiff resistance rom the 31st Rifle Brigade. Snowdrifts and freezing winds further reduced German tactical mobility. Brandenberger's burnt-out division was so imited in firepower and mobility that it not only failed to punch through a ingle Soviet brigade, but it suffered heavy casualties. Oberst von Wagner's Panzergrenadier-Regiment 8 suffered 286 casualties in the first 24 hours of he attack, or nearly 30 per cent losses. However, the attack of 8.Panzer-Division was not without effect, since it caused Galitski to defer large-scale ttacks upon Velikiye Luki, and he decided to transfer the 44th Ski Brigade und the 26th Rifle Brigade from the Kholm sector to reinforce the 31st Rifle Brigade. Galitski was determined to stop any German relief effort. Meanwhile, Maslov's 381st Rifle Division and Lebedev's 18th Mechanized Brigade began their attack upon Novosokolniki, but could not make any real progress against Scherer's improvised defences. Both Brandenberger's attack und the Soviet attack on Novosokolniki continued on 30 November, but uchieved little. The 8.Panzer-Division managed to advance a total of about 5km into a narrow salient, but could not even reach Lake Kisloye, 12km north-west of Velikiye Luki. By the end of 30 November, it was clear that he Soviet bid to capture Novosokolniki had failed, and likewise 8.Panzer-Division was too weak to reach Velikiye Luki.

In the centre, Gruppe Meyer continued to hold on, but it was hard-pressed by continuous small-scale Soviet attacks and bombardment. All 15 assault guns provided to Meyer just before the Soviet offensive began had now exhausted their fuel and ammunition. Gruppe Klatt and Giehl's Grenadier-Regiment 251 continued to fend off Soviet attacks against Chernosem station, but their combined combat strength was now just 1,200 infantrymen n four battalions and eight assault guns. The Jäger-Bataillon 3, holding south of Chernosem, was reduced to just 130 troops. Klatt managed to mount some local counter-attacks, but he could not affect a link-up with either Gruppe Meyer or Gruppe Häheler advancing along the rail line. Gruppe Jaschke, with a mixed force of five battalions, was able to slowly push its way up the Nevel–Mart'yanovo road, which reduced the threat that Gruppe Schröder would be surrounded. However, the German situation on the ground was extremely tenuous due to heavy casualties and limited supplies. Generalleutnant Werner Göritz's 291.Infanterie-Division was arriving slowly, und thus far Heeresgruppe Mitte had not agreed to release the entire division to Gruppe Chevallerie. Luftwaffe air support was minimal due to low cloud

cover and frequent periods of sleet and rain. Although the garrison in Velikiye Luki was not yet hard-pressed, aerial resupply was unavailable and von der Chevallerie realized that even rescuing Gruppe Meyer was going to be difficult with the available forces. Von Kluge concurred and favoured a tactical withdrawal to save what could be saved, but an order from Hitler on the evening of 29 November removed any possibility of tactical flexibility. 'Combat operations in the Velikiye Luki area are to be conducted so that contact with individual *Kampfgruppen* can be re-established. A withdrawal to the west is out of the question.'

Exhausted German troops sleep until the next push. The German infantry in the relief force was quickly exhausted by the terrain, weather, lack of sleep and the intensity of enemy resistance. Many of the new infantry replacements had not been as well trained as previous German infantry and had difficulty facing up to the rigours of protracted winter combat. (Nik Cornish at www. Stavka.org.uk)

On the Soviet side, Galitski began feeding the rest of Korchagin's 2nd Mechanized Corps into the battle; he sent the 33rd Tank Brigade to support Lebedev's 18th Mechanized Brigade at Novosokolniki and the 34th Mechanized Brigade and 36th Tank Brigade to block 8.Panzer-Division. The 43rd Mechanized Brigade was sent to reinforce 9th Guards Rifle Division's attacks on Gruppe Klatt. Obviously splitting up 2nd Mechanized Corps was not a very sound decision, since it scattered the 3rd Shock Army's most powerful reserve, but Galitski decided to 'play it safe' rather than risk the Germans reaching Velikiye Luki. He also decided to request additional reinforcement from Purkayev's Kalinin Front. As yet, no serious attack had been made on the encircled garrison in Velikiye Luki, and Galitski decided that the priority was to stop the relief attempts by 8.Panzer-Division and Gruppe Jaschke, then crush Gruppe Meyer and Gruppe Klatt.

THE INITIAL GERMAN RELIEF EFFORTS, 1–12 DECEMBER 1942

As a result of Hitler's order, von der Chevallerie was obliged to continue attacking with completely inadequate forces in miserable weather, as well as to hold on to a number of vulnerable positions. On 1 December, a single reinforced battalion (III./Grenadier-Regiment 76) managed to link up with Gruppe Klatt, south of Chernosem station. After repairing damaged sections of track, the Germans were even able to run a supply train up to Chernosem to resupply Klatt's Gebirgsjäger and Giehl's Grenadier-Regiment 251. The train carried vital ammunition, food, fuel and medical supplies. Once resupplied, Klatt intended to try to push north to link up with Gruppe Meyer, which reported by radio that it was extremely short of ammunition. Klatt was provided with all the firepower available, including more assault guns from Sturmgeschütz-Abteilung 185 and Sturmgeschütz-Batterie 459, Nebelwerfer from III./Werfer-Regiment 55, as well as three artillery battalions. However, the rest of Gruppe Jaschke was tied up supporting Gruppe Schröder, which had been compressed into a 4km x 2km salient against the Lovat River. The positions held by Gruppe Schröder were now irrelevant, but von der

The initial German reaction, 29 November–8 December 1942

N

Informal organizational structure

5 miles

5km

Lukino

Mulina

Gorochov'ye

Velikiye Luki

257

277

Bulynino

Kupuy

28 (-)

Porech'ye

Mart'yanovo

Gruppe Schröder

SEP

Polibino

184

4

357

1261

III

Gribushino

Chusprovo

6

Meyer

43

9 Gd

Bogoroditskoye

Kostelevo

46 Gd

Polom

285

III

Gruppe Jaschke

Komzha

Lovat

Gorovatka

31

Gritskovo

Lake Kisloye

34

36

9

Olkhovo

Demya

257

Fedkovo

Markovo

7

Leshakovo

ChernoSem

139

Klatt

21 Gd

3

8

Gorki

381 (-)

2

18

33

Lovno

291

10

III/76

Opukhliki

3

Novosokolniki

8

Great Ivan Lake

Nevel

1. 29 November 1942: 8.Panzer-Division attacks at Gorki and pushes east against the Soviet 31st Rifle Brigade, but suffers heavy losses.
2. 29–30 November: the 381st Rifle Division and 18th Mechanized Brigade launch probing attacks against outer defences of Novosokolniki, but make no progress. They are reinforced by the 33rd Tank Brigade.
3. 29–30 November: Gruppe Jaschke deploys to reinforce Gruppe Schröder.
4. 29 November–3 December: the 21st Guards Rifle Division, 28th Division and 184th Tank Brigade make repeated attacks on Gruppe Schröder.
5. 1 December: Gruppe Häheler establishes contact with Gruppe Klatt and the rail line is cleared up to Chernosem station.
6. 1–5 December: the 9th Guards Rifle Division, 357th Rifle Division and 43rd Mechanized Brigade make repeated attacks on the encircled Gruppe Meyer.
7. 3–5 December: Gruppe Klatt establishes a tenuous link with Gruppe Meyer. Over the next 24 hours, Meyer evacuates his personnel but destroys his heavy equipment.
8. 5–8 December: Scherer creates alarm units south of Novosokolniki to block Soviet infiltration south of the city.
9. 6 December: the 36th Tank Brigade unsuccessfully counter-attacks 8.Panzer-Division.
10. 8 December: the lead elements of 291.Infanterie-Division begin assembling south of Leshakovo.

47

A German 21cm Mörser 18. The Germans had one battery with three of these pieces in Velikiye Luki and the relief forces were provided with two Mörser 18 batteries. The Mörser 18 could fire a 113kg high-explosive shell out to a maximum range of 16km. However, this 16-ton howitzer was difficult to move around a winter battlefield and had a low rate of fire. (Nik Cornish at www.Stavka.org.uk)

Chevallerie was reluctant to abandon them after Hitler's order. Nor did the weather favour a relief operation at this point, alternating between cold frost one day and rain or sleet the next day, which reduced German mobility and prevented the Luftwaffe from providing much help. Von Greim managed to provide a few Ju-87 Stuka sorties from III./Sturzkampfgeschwader 71 to bomb Soviet artillery positions near Velikiye Luki, but these were too few to influence the battle.

On 2 December, Klatt began pushing north against elements of Prostiakov's 9th Guards Rifle Division in an effort to reach Gruppe Meyer before it was destroyed. If any troops could move and attack under these winter conditions, it was Klatt's Gebirgsjäger, but they were badly worn down by eight days of continuous combat. Nevertheless, on 3 December, Klatt's Gebirgsjäger achieved a tenuous link-up with Meyer's troops near the village of Botovo. Out of Gruppe Meyer's original combat strength of 1,220 men, fewer than 300 were still on their feet and 500 were wounded. All of Meyer's motor transport was either destroyed or out of fuel. During the night of 3/4 December, the Germans were able to evacuate most of the wounded, but Beloborodov's Guards rifle corps noticed the link-up and mounted a full-scale attack with 9th Guards Rifle Division, 46th Guards Rifle Division and elements of 2nd Mechanized Corps on the morning of 5 December, which severed the link between Gruppe Meyer and Gruppe Klatt. Facing annihilation, the survivors of Gruppe Meyer managed to reach Gruppe Klatt after dark, but they were forced to abandon all of their heavy equipment. In addition to the decimation of three infantry battalions, Gruppe Meyer lost 234 machine guns, 51 mortars, 32 anti-tank guns, 17 artillery pieces, 36 Nebelwerfer and 12 assault guns. Nor did Gruppe Klatt escape unscathed: it lost an additional 191 machine guns, 10 mortars, 28 anti-tank guns, six artillery pieces and 13 assault guns. The survivors of both groups fell back towards Chernosem station. Soviet-era histories claim that Gruppe Meyer was destroyed – which is nearly true – but the fact that the survivors escaped does not alter the fact that Scherer's 83.Infanterie-Division had been decimated and lost most of its heavy weapons.

Soviet losses in the battle to reduce Gruppe Meyer were also very heavy, and the Germans claimed that the effort cost 5th Guards Rifle Corps about 5,000 dead and 87 tanks knocked out. The Sturmgeschütz crews claimed 36 tank kills and the Panzerjäger another 20, with the rest destroyed by artillery and close combat. One German soldier, Gefreiter Werner Wrangel, a gunner in 1./Panzerjäger-Abteilung 183, was awarded the Ritterkreuz des Eisernen Kreuzes for destroying 17 enemy tanks. Based upon Soviet prisoner reports, Prostiakov's 9th Guards Rifle Division had been decimated and was now nearly combat ineffective. On the other hand, German losses were also debilitating; Sturmgeschutz-Abteilung 185 had lost 25 of its 29 assault guns and suffered over 90 casualties, while 291.Infanterie-Division's elements had suffered over 400 casualties in just two days of combat. The Panzer *Kompanie* on loan from 12.Panzer-Division, 8./Panzer-Regiment 29, had been badly knocked about after a tank battle with Soviet KV-1s near the bridge at Stukany; only one of its 11 PzKpfw IV tanks were still operational.

Von der Chevallerie pressed Heeresgruppe Mitte and OKH for more reinforcements. With 83.Infanterie-Division no longer combat worthy, von Kluge finally agreed to release the rest of Göritz's 291. Infanterie-Division to Gruppe Chevallerie, as well as 1.SS-Infanterie-Brigade (mot.). The OKH provided 6.Luftwaffen-Feld-Division, one of the newly created ground units formed by the Luftwaffe from excess personnel; the division had just four infantry and one artillery battalion. Although the Luftwaffe ground units lacked the experience and training of the Heer divisions, Reichsmarschall Hermann Göring had ensured that they were very well equipped; for example, the *Feld-Divisionen* were outfitted with all brand-new MG 42 machine guns (instead of the older German, Czech and Russian machine guns that Scherer's infantrymen possessed) and it was given modern 7.5cm anti-tank guns. Once 6.Luftwaffen-Feld-Division arrived in Nevel, it was deployed east of Opukhliki, to reinforce the sector held by Gruppe Schröder. Both sides continued the useless fighting along the Nevel–Mart'yanovo road, with the Soviets obsessed with capturing the strongpoints in the villages of Polibino and Porech'ye. By 2 December, Kniazkov's 28th Rifle Division was in poor shape from heavy losses, and it was reinforced with the fresh 45th Ski Brigade. Although this infusion of fresh Soviet troops caused trouble for the Germans in this sector, it diverted valuable troops away from the main objective of taking Velikiye Luki.

After Gruppe Meyer was relieved, the Germans began to shift their units around Chernosem station to create a more coherent defence and to prepare for another relief effort towards Velikiye Luki. Some of the remnants of Scherer's 83.Infanterie-Division moved to Novosokolniki to regroup and strengthen the defence of that city, while Gruppe Klatt continued to anchor the line at Chernosem. Gruppe Jaschke detached one *Kampfgruppe* from 20.Infanterie-Division (mot.) to reinforce Brandenberger's 8.Panzer-Division, but incorporated those elements of Göritz's 291.Infanterie-Division that were on hand and SS-Oberführer Karl Hermann's infantry brigade. Unfortunately, von der Chevallerie continued to reinforce his right flank, while leaving his centre and left flank under-resourced. He put Scherer in charge of organizing the forces located between Chernosem and Novosokolniki to create a patchwork front line. Several alarm units, such as Alarm-Bataillon Schön, were created from rear-echelon troops to create a thin screening force south-east of Novosokolniki. Amazingly, Galitski made no effort to interfere with these German tactical redeployments.

North-west of Velikiye Luki, Brandenberger's 8.Panzer-Division could only mount short offensive jabs due to its limited strength. Galitski reinforced

A German PzKpfw III command tank pauses near a field radio station. The relief forces had relatively few tanks, and among the few they did have were a number of short-barrelled PzKpfw III and PzKpfw IV tanks. The command tanks were useful as mobile command posts and helped protect key leaders from enemy artillery fire. Note the chopped firewood, indicating that the command post intends to occupy this position for a while. (Nik Cornish at www. Stavka.org.uk)

A German infantry company forms up in preparation for a relief attack towards Velikiye Luki, December 1942. Gruppe Wöhler was handicapped by its shortage of infantrymen throughout the campaign, and units such as this suffered heavy losses due to enemy artillery fire. (Süddeutsche Zeitung Bild 00398212, Foto: Scherl)

this sector with the 26th Rifle Brigade and 44th Ski Brigade which made it even more difficult for Brandenberger to continue attacking. Galitski also decided to commit some armour to this sector to stop any further German advance. On 6 December, Polkovnik Maksim I. Pakhomov's 36th Tank Brigade from 2nd Mechanized Corps launched a surprise counter-attack against 8.Panzer-Division, complete with heavy artillery support and sorties from Il-2 Sturmoviks. Rather than go toe to toe with superior enemy armour, Brandenberger pulled his thin-skinned Pz. 38(t) light tanks back. For his part, Pakhomov committed less than half his tanks. Pakhomov's tanks managed to inflict 37 casualties upon Panzergrenadier-Regiment 8, but a pair of Marder II self-propelled anti-tank guns from Panzerjäger-Abteilung 43 knocked out five Soviet tanks, which caused the rest to retreat. The Germans also admitted the loss of two Schützenpanzerwagen (SPW) half-tracks and two anti-tank guns. Rather than launch one all-out attack, Pakhomov continued to launch company-size tank attacks over the next several days, which enabled Brandenberger's Panzerjägers to pick them off a few at a time; by 9 December, the 36th Tank Brigade had lost 35 of its 49 tanks. Nevertheless, Brandenberger's 8.Panzer-Division had effectively been halted 20km short of Velikiye Luki. In order to assist 8.Panzer-Division in holding on to the ground already recaptured, Gruppe Jaschke transferred its *Kradschützen* (motorcycle infantry) battalion to Brandenberger.

Von der Chevallerie and Scherer decided to make a push towards Velikiye Luki from the south-west as soon as sufficient forces were available. Instead of pushing straight up the rail line to Velikiye Luki, von der Chevallerie opted to make his relief operation 5km west of the line, in order to bypass the strongest Soviet defences. By the evening of 8 December, Göritz had four infantry battalions from his division assembled south of Leshakovo, along with some artillery and a few assault guns. In military terms, this is known as a 'rock soup offensive' that uses whatever elements are available – typically a method only appropriate in extremis. At dawn on 9 December, Göritz attacked and was able to advance a few kilometres against light resistance before he had to halt. Galitski positioned Prostiakov's 9th Guards Rifle Division to block the German advance and even mounted local counter-attacks to keep the enemy off balance. Göritz, with some help from Gruppe Klatt, continued to make minor gains on 10 and 11 December, but was only able to clear Leshakovo and Suragino by 12 December. The Soviet 9th Guards Rifle Division elements defending this sector were burnt out from fighting Gruppe Meyer; the 3rd Battalion, 22nd Rifle Regiment had just 72 soldiers left to hold a 4km-wide sector near Leshakovo. However, Galitski shifted elements of Lebedev's 18th Mechanized Brigade and the 44th Ski

Brigade to stop the German advance. Lebedev's brigade still had a dozen tanks and the 44th Ski Brigade some 1,300 light infantry, which was enough to stop four German battalions. In four days of attacking, 291.Infanterie-Division advanced only 4km and still had strong Soviet forces on both its flanks. Furthermore, 291.Infanterie-Division still had not received its missing regiment, which had run into trouble near Nevel; Soviet partisans laid mines on the rail tracks and scored a major success when the lead train carrying Grenadier-Regiment 504 ran over a mine; the regimental commander, Oberst Botho von Frantzius, was killed and most of his staff were injured. Even once the two additional battalions of Grenadier-Regiment 504 reached the front, the division was extremely short of combat leaders. The attempted relief operation had accomplished very little except grinding down some of the few remaining German combat-effective units, and Göritz's forward positions were still 17km from Velikiye Luki. The first German attempts to reach the encircled garrison in Velikiye Luki had failed.

THE SIEGE OF VELIKIYE LUKI, 27 NOVEMBER–18 DECEMBER 1942

Oberstleutnant von Sass' garrison in Velikiye Luki passed the first two weeks of the siege without seeing substantial combat. Once the city was surrounded by Polkovnik Anatoly A. Dyakonov's 257th Rifle Division and Polkovnik Aleksandr L. Kronik's 357th Rifle Division, the Soviets focused on tightening the noose, rather than launching an immediate assault. Both divisions began the battle significantly understrength and had no great numerical superiority over the German garrison. Initially, the Soviets conducted probing attacks against Velikiye Luki's outer positions while constructing a ring of fieldworks around the city. For the first week, Soviet attacks were only conducted in company- or battalion-size strength, although casualties quickly mounted. Both Soviet divisions formed mixed 100-man assault detachments, which included infantry and sappers. The most exposed German positions – Wesel in the west and Bayreuth and the Felt Factory in the south-west – were virtually cut off from the main garrison. Von Sass used his heavy artillery to harass Soviet movements, and his 10cm battery (4./Artillerie-Regiment 70) regularly pounded assembly areas. However, the German artillery had a limited ammunition supply and due to poor weather the Luftwaffe was unable to provide any significant aerial resupply until mid-December. On 6 December, the Luftwaffe managed to deliver about 4 tons of supplies via parachute containers, but most days there was nothing. On that day, von Sass informed Scherer that the garrison still had 18 days' worth of food, but less than ten days' worth of ammunition.

The Soviets made their first major attack on the city at 1000hrs on 10 December, when two battalions from Kronik's 357th Rifle Division advanced against the western sector, supported by Katyusha MRL barrages. The Soviet infantry was able to reach some of the German positions, but was ejected after close-quarter fighting. In order to soften up the defences, a regiment of Pe-2s from General-mayor Vladimir A. Sudets' 1st Bomber Aviation Corps appeared over the city and dropped 300 bombs, one of which hit the main German aid station. On 11 December, 357th Rifle Division continued attacking the western suburbs with infantry and tanks, while Dyakonov's 257th Rifle Division

A German column with infantry and PzKpfw III tanks moves to an assembly area in preparation for the first attempt to relieve Velikiye Luki, December 1942. Gruppe Wöhler had difficulty massing combat power to form a real *Schwerpunkt* (main effort) capable of conducting a sustained drive towards Velikiye Luki. (Süddeutsche Zeitung Bild 00398215, Foto: Scherl)

mounted a large attack against the Felt Factory in the south-west. The German defences held, thanks to the defensive firepower of their machine guns and artillery, as well as ability of the fortified strongpoints to absorb punishment. German Nebelwerfer rockets were devastating against Soviet troops caught in the open. At least two Soviet tanks were knocked out, including one by a German grenadier who used a T-miner in close combat. Nevertheless, Soviet attacks continued in both sectors on 12 December, without any gain. Von Sass' artillery used up a considerable amount of its ammunition in repelling these assaults, including 2,800 10.5cm and 900 15cm rounds, as well as 425 Nebelwerfer rockets.

In fact, these three days of attacks were merely the preliminary for Galitski's main event, which was an all-out assault against Velikiye Luki that began at 0800hrs on 13 December. An artillery preparation from 566 guns and mortars preceded the assault. For the first time, Dyakonov committed all three regiments from 257th Rifle Division to attack the north-west sector while Kronik committed his three regiments from 357th Rifle Division against the western sector. Von Sass immediately requested Stuka sorties, but the Luftwaffe could provide none due to overcast skies and fog. Led by tanks, 257th Rifle Division penetrated the thin German line near Stützpunkt Hamburg and pushed into the city outskirts. From his command post near the rail station, von Sass tried to orchestrate a counter-attack – which failed to evict Kronik's troops. By mid-afternoon, von Sass was shaken by the power of the Soviet attack and radioed several panicky messages to Scherer. Von Kluge himself intervened, radioing to von Sass: 'Help is coming!' Scherer suspected that von Sass was conducting an unimaginative defence, since the eastern sector of the city was not under serious attack and he should have been able to shift some troops to the western sector. Although some Soviet tanks and infantry reached the Lovat, the German infantry managed to hold on to the key positions and inflict heavy losses on the enemy.

Galitski kept up the pressure on the morning of 14 December, with 257th Rifle Division expanding its positions near Stützpunkt Hamburg. After another bombardment by heavy artillery, Kronik's troops succeeded in capturing Hamburg – the first major German position in Velikiye Luki to be lost. German Panzerjäger succeeded in destroying four Soviet tanks, but a battery of 15cm howitzers was overrun. Due to poor weather, the Luftwaffe was not able to intervene until noon, with Stukas belatedly bombing Kronik's assembly areas west of the city. Soviet aircraft also continued to bomb the German garrison, although fighters from 11./Jagdgeschwader 51 managed to shoot down two Il-2 Sturmoviks near Velikiye Luki. The German garrison still held the Citadel and a few positions west of the Lovat, but the Soviet attacks were now slowly gaining ground. Amazingly, the German company

(Oberleutnant Weihe's 2./Grenadier-Regiment 277) in Stützpunkt Wesel, which lay west of the city, was still holding out. Von Sass ordered this company to abandon their position and Weihe's men were somehow able to infiltrate through Soviet lines and reach the Citadel during the night of 14/15 December.

Another powerful assault in the western sector of Velikiye Luki began on the morning of 15 December, and made steady progress. Von Sass reported that his losses were 'enormous' and stated that by noon, 'without Stukas the situation is hopeless'. While German losses in men and material had been serious, they did not exceed 10 per cent and it seemed to Scherer and von Kluge that von Sass had poor situational awareness. After the battle, a German survivor, Feldwebel Karl Kolle from 6./Grenadier-Regiment 277, reported that his company had suffered relatively few casualties up to this point in the battle and that on 15 December his unit repulsed all enemy attacks and inflicted over 100 dead. Feldwebel Kolle also reported that 23 Soviet troops deserted to his company on this day, indicating the fragility of morale in some Soviet units. Nevertheless, Soviet tanks were able to reach the Lovat, and the railroad bridge 800m south of the Citadel was captured (the Germans retained control over the 24-ton bridge, north-east of the Citadel). At 1255hrs, the Soviets sent a delegation towards the Citadel under a flag of truce, offering surrender terms; von Sass rejected them. Scherer and von Kluge both chastised von Sass via radio, ordering him to desist from panicky reports and to provide them with reliable information. Subsequently, von Sass directed the creation of a new line along the Lovat, but German troops in the Citadel were now nearly isolated.

After the rejection of his surrender offer, Galitski decided to treat the German garrison to a heavy dose of Soviet firepower on 16 December, including continuous attacks by 3rd Air Army bombers, heavy artillery and multiple rocket-launchers. Pe-2 bombers from the 263rd Bomber Aviation Division dropped 13 tons of bombs on the city, plus leaflets. The Luftwaffe made an appearance over the city, with He-111s dropping 10.4 tons of ammunition while a surge of fighter sorties from III./Jagdgeschwader 51 and 7./Jagdgeschwader 54 claimed 12 Soviet aircraft in the Velikiye Luki sector, including seven fighters and five Il-2 Sturmoviks. Apparently, the nervousness about the situation in Velikiye Luki reached all the way up to Hitler's headquarters at the Wolfsschanze (Wolf's Lair) in East Prussia. At 2200hrs, von Sass received a direct message from the Führer himself, which stated: 'I express my appreciation to you and your soldiers for their bravery. I am convinced that you will hold like iron, as General Scherer did in Kholm, until you are relieved.'

By throwing support troops into the line as infantry, von Sass was able to create a new defensive perimeter, which held. In four days of fighting, the garrison had suffered about 700 casualties and had lost one-third of

German infantry struggle to move a light artillery piece across the snow without benefit of horses or vehicles. Most of the German units involved in the relief of Velikiye Luki had very little motor transport and relied upon horses and manpower to move equipment near the front line. (Nik Cornish at www.Stavka.org.uk)

THE SOVIET ASSAULT INTO VELIKIYE LUKI, 13–31 DECEMBER 1942

The 3rd Shock Army began its assault upon Velikiye Luki with the 257th Rifle Division and 357th Rifle Division on 10 December 1942, but initially the German garrison repulsed all attacks. However, as the Soviets fed more troops into the battle, the Germans began to lose one defensive position after another until the garrison was finally split into two fragments.

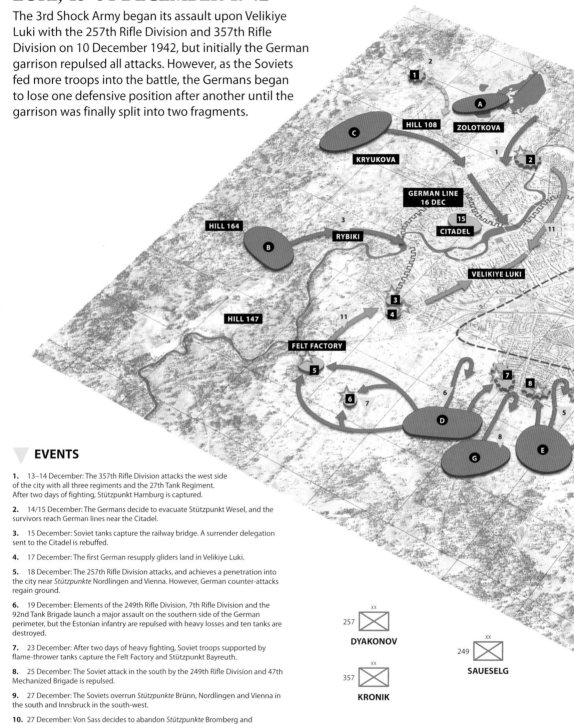

▼ EVENTS

1. 13–14 December: The 357th Rifle Division attacks the west side of the city with all three regiments and the 27th Tank Regiment. After two days of fighting, Stützpunkt Hamburg is captured.

2. 14/15 December: The Germans decide to evacuate Stützpunkt Wesel, and the survivors reach German lines near the Citadel.

3. 15 December: Soviet tanks capture the railway bridge. A surrender delegation sent to the Citadel is rebuffed.

4. 17 December: The first German resupply gliders land in Velikiye Luki.

5. 18 December: The 257th Rifle Division attacks, and achieves a penetration into the city near *Stützpunkte* Nordlingen and Vienna. However, German counter-attacks regain ground.

6. 19 December: Elements of the 249th Rifle Division, 7th Rifle Division and the 92nd Tank Brigade launch a major assault on the southern side of the German perimeter, but the Estonian infantry are repulsed with heavy losses and ten tanks are destroyed.

7. 23 December: After two days of heavy fighting, Soviet troops supported by flame-thrower tanks capture the Felt Factory and Stützpunkt Bayreuth.

8. 25 December: The Soviet attack in the south by the 249th Rifle Division and 47th Mechanized Brigade is repulsed.

9. 27 December: The Soviets overrun *Stützpunkte* Brünn, Nordlingen and Vienna in the south and Innsbruck in the south-west.

10. 27 December: Von Sass decides to abandon *Stützpunkte* Bromberg and Brandenberg in order to concentrate his remaining troops around the rail station.

11. 30 December: The Soviets overrun Stützpunkt Würzburg in the south, while elements of the 357th Rifle Division and tanks break through on the east side of the Lovat and begin to push towards the city centre. By late afternoon, the Soviet pincers have linked up and isolated the German troops in the Citadel.

xx
257 ⊠
DYAKONOV

xx
357 ⊠
KRONIK

xx
249 ⊠
SAUESELG

Note: gridlines are shown at intervals of 1km (0.62 miles)

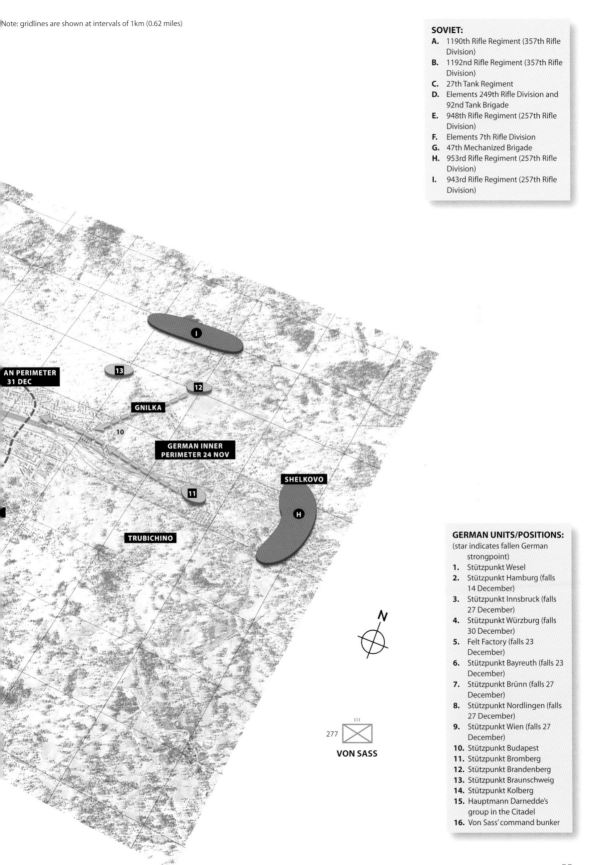

SOVIET:
A. 1190th Rifle Regiment (357th Rifle Division)
B. 1192nd Rifle Regiment (357th Rifle Division)
C. 27th Tank Regiment
D. Elements 249th Rifle Division and 92nd Tank Brigade
E. 948th Rifle Regiment (257th Rifle Division)
F. Elements 7th Rifle Division
G. 47th Mechanized Brigade
H. 953rd Rifle Regiment (257th Rifle Division)
I. 943rd Rifle Regiment (257th Rifle Division)

GERMAN UNITS/POSITIONS:
(star indicates fallen German strongpoint)
1. Stützpunkt Wesel
2. Stützpunkt Hamburg (falls 14 December)
3. Stützpunkt Innsbruck (falls 27 December)
4. Stützpunkt Würzburg (falls 30 December)
5. Felt Factory (falls 23 December)
6. Stützpunkt Bayreuth (falls 23 December)
7. Stützpunkt Brünn (falls 27 December)
8. Stützpunkt Nordlingen (falls 27 December)
9. Stützpunkt Wien (falls 27 December)
10. Stützpunkt Budapest
11. Stützpunkt Bromberg
12. Stützpunkt Brandenberg
13. Stützpunkt Braunschweig
14. Stützpunkt Kolberg
15. Hauptmann Darnedde's group in the Citadel
16. Von Sass' command bunker

AN PERIMETER 31 DEC

GNILKA

GERMAN INNER PERIMETER 24 NOV

SHELKOVO

TRUBICHINO

277 VON SASS

its artillery, but was still combat effective. Although von Sass could not see it, Soviet losses of infantry had been crippling, and no major attacks were launched on 17 December. Instead, Galitski used his superiority in artillery and airpower to bombard Velikiye Luki throughout the day. The city was being relentlessly pounded into rubble. Luftwaffe fighters claimed another five Soviet aircraft, but 3rd Air Army was able to maintain air superiority over Velikiye Luki most of the time. The Luftwaffe also succeeded in landing the first Go 242 glider in Velikiye Luki, with three tons of medical supplies – a tenuous link had been established with the garrison.

Galitski renewed his ground offensive on 18 December, but shifted to the southern sector against the Nordlingen and Vienna *Stützpunkten*. Soviet artillery bombarded the city with over 15,000 rounds, including for the first time some 203mm shells. Dyakonov's 257th Rifle Division attacked with 50 tanks, and managed to penetrate between the German strongpoints. Von Sass ordered a counter-attack, but this failed to evict the Soviet troops. Much of the fighting was at close quarters, in shattered buildings. Yet even minor gains cost the attackers another 2,500 casualties and five tanks, which quickly depleted the assault units. After six days of intense urban combat, the front-line soldiers on both sides in Velikiye Luki were exhausted. The city itself was now a shattered, burning wreck, with rubble and craters making any kind of tactical movement difficult. The Red Army was learning just how difficult it was to capture a fortified city, while German senior commanders were learning how difficult it was to conduct battles via radio.

GRUPPE WÖHLER'S RELIEF EFFORT FLOUNDERS, 15–22 DECEMBER 1942

Events developing elsewhere on the Eastern Front had a major impact on the German and Soviet responses to the crisis at Velikiye Luki. Despite some tense moments, Model's 9.Armee had succeeded in stopping Operation *Mars* and by early December, German counter-attacks had isolated the spearheads of the two Soviet pincer groups. Soviet losses were catastrophic and a large portion of the Kalinin Front's 41st Army was encircled near Belyi. However, Zhukov had not yet given up on Operation *Mars* and continued to mount desperation attacks, if nothing else, to pin down von Kluge's mobile reserves. On the German side, von Kluge was cautious, preferring to finish off the trapped 41st Army and keep all his Panzer units in hand until he was certain that the Soviet offensive against the Rzhev salient had ended. Von Kluge was also concerned that the Soviet 4th Shock Army might try to make another effort to seize Velizh and Demidov, so he wanted to keep some reserves in this sector – even though it was not under attack. Major Heinrich Pricken's I./Panzer-Regiment 15 (part of 11.Panzer-Division, but temporarily serving as an independent tank battalion), which had 33 tanks, was stationed near Demidov. Von der Chevallerie had made multiple requests for this battalion to be assigned to his command to spearhead the relief effort, but von Kluge refused to part with it. The Luftwaffe's elite 7.Flieger-Division, which had six *Fallschirmjäger* battalions, was also holding a quiet sector of the line near Demidov. Von der Chevallerie pleaded for even one of these elite battalions to assist his relief operation, but Reichsmarschall Hermann Göring personally quashed this request.

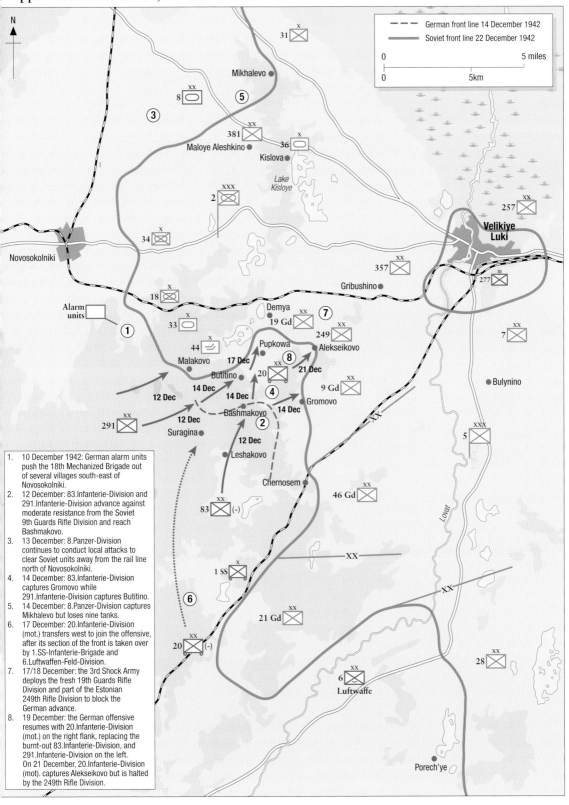

Legend:
- – – – German front line 14 December 1942
- ▓▓▓ Soviet front line 22 December 1942

0 ——————— 5 miles
0 ——————— 5km

N ▲

Mikhalevo ●

8 ⊏XX⊐ ③

⑤

381 ⊏XX⊐
Maloye Aleshkino ●   36 ⊏X⊐
Kislova ●

31 ⊏X⊐

Lake Kisloye

2 ⊏XXX⊐

34 ⊏X⊐

Novosokolniki

18 ⊏X⊐

257 ⊏XX⊐

Velikiye Luki

357 ⊏XX⊐
Gribushino ●   277 ⊏III⊐

Alarm units ⊏ ⊐ ①

33 ⊏X⊐   Demya ●
44 ⊏X⊐   19 Gd ⊏X⊐ ⑦   7 ⊏XX⊐

Pupkowa ●   249 ⊏XX⊐
Malakovo ●   Alekseikovo ●
17 Dec   ⑧
Butitino ●   20 ⊏XX⊐   21 Dec
14 Dec   ④   14 Dec   9 Gd ⊏XX⊐
12 Dec   14 Dec   Bashmakovo   Gromovo ●   Bulynino ●
291 ⊏XX⊐   ②
Suragina ●   12 Dec
12 Dec   Leshakovo ●   5 ⊏XXX⊐

83 ⊏XX⊐ (-)   Chernosem ●   46 Gd ⊏XX⊐

XX

1 SS ⊏X⊐

⑥   21 Gd ⊏XX⊐

20 ⊏XX⊐ (-)   28 ⊏XX⊐

6 ⊏XX⊐
Luftwaffe

Porech'ye ○

1. 10 December 1942: German alarm units push the 18th Mechanized Brigade out of several villages south-east of Novosokolniki.
2. 12 December: 83.Infanterie-Division and 291.Infanterie-Division advance against moderate resistance from the Soviet 9th Guards Rifle Division and reach Bashmakovo.
3. 13 December: 8.Panzer-Division continues to conduct local attacks to clear Soviet units away from the rail line north of Novosokolniki.
4. 14 December: 83.Infanterie-Division captures Gromovo while 291.Infanterie-Division captures Butitino.
5. 14 December: 8.Panzer-Division captures Mikhalevo but loses nine tanks.
6. 17 December: 20.Infanterie-Division (mot.) transfers west to join the offensive, after its section of the front is taken over by 1.SS-Infanterie-Brigade and 6.Luftwaffen-Feld-Division.
7. 17/18 December: the 3rd Shock Army deploys the fresh 19th Guards Rifle Division and part of the Estonian 249th Rifle Division to block the German advance.
8. 19 December: the German offensive resumes with 20.Infanterie-Division (mot.) on the right flank, replacing the burnt-out 83.Infanterie-Division, and 291.Infanterie-Division on the left. On 21 December, 20.Infanterie-Division (mot.) captures Alekseikovo but is halted by the 249th Rifle Division.

A number of Soviet troops – particularly Estonians – continued to desert to the Germans, and some worked willingly with the enemy as so-called 'Hiwis' (short for Hilfswilliger, or volunteer assistant). This Soviet soldier appears to be helping the Germans to lay signal wire to a forward position, allegedly near the village of Botovo. The Germans found that these defectors could be quite useful, and most German units by 1942 had significant numbers of Hiwis. At least 60 Hiwis were part of the garrison in Velikiye Luki. (Author's collection)

Reports from the Demyansk sector were also encouraging since it was evident by early December that the Soviet North West Front's offensive against the Ramushevo corridor had failed once again to isolate the German salient. Yet von Küchler was just as cautious as von Kluge and refused to release any more reserves from Heeresgruppe Nord until the Soviet offensive had ended. In southern Russian, von Manstein's newly formed Heeresgruppe Don began Operation *Wintergewitter* on 12 December, the effort to rescue the encircled 6.Armee at Stalingrad. From the OKH perspective, the priority was Stalingrad and the Rzhev and Demyansk sectors were past the point of crisis, so any reinforcements from the west would go to von Manstein. From the Stavka perspective, the Demyansk and Rzhev operations had failed, but Zhukov wanted to continue fighting in the Rzhev, Velikiye Luki and Demyansk sectors for as long as possible – even if it had little chance of success – to prevent the Germans from transferring any units to reinforce von Manstein's Heeresgruppe Don.

After the failure of Gruppe Chevallerie's initial attempts to relieve the encircled garrison in Velikiye Luki, von Kluge re-examined the situation. He decided to send his chief of staff, Generalleutnant Otto Wöhler, to lead another relief operation. On the morning of 15 December, Wöhler arrived with six staff officers in Lovno to take command of the relief operation; the effort would be run from a rustic barn in the middle of nowhere. With considerable reluctance, von Kluge finally agreed to release Major Pricken's I./Panzer-Regiment 15 to join the operation. Gruppe Wöhler was expected to pull together the various German *Kampfgruppen* and mount a powerful offensive to rescue the garrison of Velikiye Luki. However, Wöhler's command consisted of 20 infantry battalions from four different divisions with an effective combat strength of fewer than 9,000 troops. All of the troops were exhausted after weeks of fighting, and the weather had turned rainy and cold, which increased cases of frostbite alarmingly. Logically Wöhler needed time to prepare these forces for a renewed offensive, but the grim reports from Velikiye Luki made it clear that Gruppe Wöhler must attack at once.

Meanwhile, Purkayev was authorized to reinforce Galitski's 3rd Shock Army in order to bring the siege of Velikiye Luki to a rapid conclusion. General-major Lembit A. Pärn's 8th Estonian Rifle Corps (7th Rifle Division, 249th Rifle Division, 19th Guards Rifle Division), which had been held in reserve near Toropets, was released to Galitski on 10 December. Except for the 19th Guards Rifle Division and the attached tank regiments, over 80 per cent of the personnel in the corps were ethnic Estonians, many of whom were not enthusiastic about serving in the Red Army. Their commander, Pärn, was a reliable Estonian communist and trained by the Soviet General

staff Academy, but possessing very limited command experience. The two divisions in the 8th Estonian Rifle Corps had spent most of 1942 in training, and were not judged ready for combat until October; they had no combat experience. Faced with the need to delay Gruppe Wöhler and finish off the German garrison in Velikiye Luki, Purkayev committed the Estonians to battle, along with the 36th Separate Tank Regiment from the RVGK.

Gruppe Wöhler attacked on 15 December, with 291.Infanterie-Division on the left and 83.Infanterie-Division on the right. Gruppe Klatt had been incorporated into Scherer's division, along with two *Jäger-Bataillone* (3 and 5). Opposing them, the Soviets had a thin screen formed by the 44th Ski Brigade, 9th Guards Rifle Division and Lebedev's 18th Mechanized Brigade (which still had 12 tanks). The axis of advance chosen lay in marshy terrain, which was now soft due to a sudden thaw. Small wooded hills were key terrain in this region, since attackers had to cross stretches of open marsh and the trails in this area were narrow and muddy. Given the nature of the terrain and the wet weather, Gruppe Wöhler only succeeded in capturing the minor village of Gromovo – a 1km gain that hardly justified the loss of hundreds more troops. Scherer's two remaining regiments were reduced to a combined battle strength of just 450 men, and one of Klatt's battalions was down to 184 men. Having lived outdoors for weeks in wet, cold conditions, Gruppe Klatt had 995 men with frostbite and the other units were in similar condition. The loss of junior leaders was particularly serious, with most companies left with only a single officer. Wöhler decided to pull Scherer's remaining troops and Gruppe Klatt out of the offensive in order to rest, which meant transferring Jaschke's still relatively strong 20.Infanterie-Division (mot.) from the right flank to the centre. The transfer was not simple and required both tactical and diplomatic finesse, since Hitler was adamant about not giving up any terrain, anywhere. Wöhler ordered 1.SS-Infanterie-Brigade (mot.) to relieve Jaschke's division on the right, so it could move to join the relief operation. With some help from von Kluge, Hitler finally allowed some shortening of the line on the right, which enabled the SS-Brigade to create a solid front. Gruppe Wöhler spent 16 and 17 December redeploying its forces and preparing for the next round.

A German soldier examines a knocked-out T-34 tank. Soviet tank losses during the Velikiye Luki operation were significant, probably about 200 tanks over the course of the six-week-long campaign. The German Panzerjäger of late 1942 were better equipped to defeat medium tanks like the T-34 than they had been in 1941. However, since the Red Army controlled the battlefield, many knocked-out tanks were eventually recovered and repaired. (Nik Cornish at www. Stavka.org.uk)

While Wöhler's troops tried to fight their way forwards through marshland, Brandenberger's 8.Panzer-Division remained stalled and facing regular Soviet counter-attacks. By 13 December, Brandenberger's division had suffered 1,473 casualties, or 43 per cent of its starting combat strength. Instead of attacking east toward Velikiye Luki, 8.Panzer-Division's remaining combat power – which was mostly its artillery – was used to clear 381st Rifle Division out of its positions north-east of Novosokolniki. Maslov's division contested every village and managed to destroy nine Pz. 38(t) tanks on 14 December. Due to Brandenberger's inability to continue advancing toward Velikiye Luki, Galitski was able to redeploy forces from west of the city to contest Gruppe Wöhler's advance. At this point in the battle, von der Chevallerie and Wöhler seriously needed to reorganize their battered forces and rethink the idea of shoving divisions up narrow forest tracks in a single pincer operation, but the situation at Velikiye Luki prevented that kind of rational approach. Prior to the Soviet offensive, von der Chevallerie had always expected to mount a relief operation from the rail hub in Novosokolniki, which presented a straight march of 21km to Velikiye Luki along good lines of communication. However, the Germans had underestimated the Soviets and relied upon expediency since the beginning of this campaign, and it was now coming back to haunt them; the only units with the ability to reach Velikiye Luki were deployed into a sector that least favoured rapid advance.

At 0800hrs on 19 December, Gruppe Wöhler resumed its advance, with Major Pricken's panzers leading the Panzergrenadiers of 20.Infanterie-Division (mot.). Wöhler was surprised to find that Galitski had reinforced this sector with General-major David M. Baranov's fresh 19th Guards Rifle Division, which had been transferred from the Western Front. The German attempt to advance on a narrow, one-tank front in wooded, marshy terrain was a mistake and Major Pricken was killed in the opening action near the village of Butitino. Snipers also killed one of the panzer company commanders with a shot to the head. Soviet artillery pummelled the trail-bound German columns, inflicting heavy losses. By the end of the day, Gruppe Wöhler had suffered 582 casualties (including 122 dead) to achieve a minor advance. Reinforced with two Jäger-Bataillone, Wöhler continued to attack on 20 December, and 291.Infanterie-Division managed to advance nearly 3km to the village of Burtseva; 69 Soviet troops were captured. However, rainy weather prevented any assistance from the Luftwaffe, and Wöhler's troops had advanced into a narrow salient that was under artillery fire from three sides. Soviet infantry had also been bypassed in the woods near Butitino and these needed to be mopped up. The German advance continued on 21 December, amidst heavy rain that reduced mobility and visibility. Supported by I./Panzer-Regiment 15, 20.Infanterie-Division (mot.) was able to capture the village of Alekseikovo, 11km from the Citadel in Velikiye Luki, but was hen stopped by a solid defence from Baranov's 249th Rifle Division. Wöhler's offensive ground to a halt on 22 December, stopped by mud, frostbite, heavy casualties and intense Soviet resistance. In four days of attacking, Wöhler had advanced only 4km. He informed von Kluge that, 'his people are finished'. Göritz's 291.Infanterie-Division had been wrecked, reduced to a combat strength of just 676 troops, while Jaschke's 20.Infanterie-Division (mot.) had about 1,000 left. Without Stuka support, Gruppe Wöhler could not silence the enemy artillery on its flanks or penetrate the labyrinth of fortified villages in its path.

After weeks of heavy fighting, the area around Velikiye Luki was littered with frozen corpses. (Nik Cornish at www. Stavka.org.uk)

While Gruppe Wöhler was inching towards Velikiye Luki, von Sass' garrison remained under heavy attack. On the morning of 19 December, Galitski committed Polkovnik Artur-Aleksandr I. Saueselg's 249th Estonian Rifle Division and the 92nd Tank Brigade (equipped with US-made Lee and Stuart tanks) to the battle along the Lovat. Despite numerical superiority, the Estonian infantry failed to gain any ground and ten tanks were destroyed. The German garrison succeeded in recovering some of the ground lost in the southern sector near Vienna. Galitski decided to pause his offensive for a day, and spent 20 December shelling the city with his heavy artillery while Gromov's 3rd Air Army relentlessly bombed the city. The German troops in Velikiye Luki lived a subterranean life, only coming out of their bunkers to repel attacks. Rations were still adequate, but ammunition stocks were running low and the troops were reaching breaking point. At 0800hrs on 21 December, the Soviets launched another major attack from the north-west, and succeeded in overrunning Stützpunkt Bremen, which had anchored the defence in that corner of the city. Galitski spent 22 December mopping up isolated German positions in the north-west. By this point, the German garrison in Velikiye Luki had been reduced to about 5,000 troops, including over 1,000 wounded.

THE BREAKING POINT, 23 DECEMBER 1942–3 JANUARY 1943

With Gruppe Wöhler halted, Galitski could turn all his attention back to crushing the German garrison in Velikiye Luki. Full-scale attacks continued in the western and southern sectors on 23 and 24 December, assisted by flame-throwing tanks. On 23 December, the Felt Factory was captured at 0950hrs, then Stützpunkt Bayreuth at 1340hrs; the loss of these positions was critical, since these were the closest positions to Gruppe Wöhler's relief forces. Galitski committed elements from both Estonian divisions to reinforce the assaults, but they proved not entirely reliable. Supposedly von Sass – who could speak Estonian – made broadcasts over a loudspeaker urging the

CHRISTMAS MORNING ATTACK, 0730HRS, 25 DECEMBER 1942 (PP. 62–63)

By late December 1942, the 3rd Shock Army gradually began to split the Velikiye Luki pocket into two smaller encirclements, by simultaneously attacking both the northern and southern flanks. Just before Christmas, the Kalinin Front committed additional infantry and a new unit – the 515th Flame-thrower Tank Battalion – which had 14 KV-8 heavy flame-thrower tanks. The Felt Factory was captured on 23 December, and the German defence was handicapped by ammunition shortages.

On Christmas morning, under the cover of thick fog, the Soviets pushed north from the Felt Factory, towards the strongpoint known as Nürnberg. The garrison's last anti-tank gun was destroyed, leaving the German infantry almost helpless against the Soviet tanks. The German defenders were particularly fearful of the enemy flame-thrower tanks. Due to the morning fog, the Russian attackers appeared suddenly at close range, giving little time for the Germans to react. Over the course of the previous month, Velikiye Luki had been shattered by thousands of round of artillery fire and the streets were littered with the dead and battlefield wreckage.

In this scene, a KV-8 (**1**) douses a German MG 34 machine-gun team (**2**, located in a shell hole beside a building) with a long jet of flame, setting the crew and their position ablaze. A few hardy German infantrymen in the building adjacent to the Soviet continue to resist (**3**), one of whom is about to hurl a concentrated charge (Geballte Ladung) at the Soviets outside. Even with flame-throwers, the Soviets must still overcome the defence of each building with intense close-quarter combat, which will cost them dearly. Although the German defence is badly stressed and nearly collapses, it somehow manages to hold on for another day. By 28 December, the Soviets will have succeeded in cutting the pocket in half, but will lack the strength to immediately conclude the battle.

Estonians not to fight for Stalin, but this claim is not verified. Most of the German artillery was very low in ammunition by this point, and the defenders had to rely upon infantry weapons to fend off attacks. Feldwebel Karl Kolle, in 6./Grenadier-Regiment 277, said the last rations from the garrison's reserves were handed out on Christmas Eve; after that, the garrison was totally dependent upon aerial resupply.

On Christmas morning, the Soviets treated the defenders to another massive artillery bombardment, including from multiple rocket-launchers, then attacked around 0800hrs with the 249th Rifle Division and Podpolkovnik Ivan F. Dremov's 47th Mechanized Brigade (which had 11 tanks). The fighting was intense and the last German 7.5cm anti-tank gun was destroyed. With most of his artillery gone or short on ammunition, von Sass used his surplus artillerymen to form assault units to mount local counter-attacks to retake any buildings that were lost. Yet for once the weather was fair, which allowed the Luftwaffe to airdrop 50 tons of supplies – just enough to prevent a collapse. Gromov's 3rd Air Army proved unsuccessful at intercepting these airdrops, but Soviet anti-aircraft firing managed to shoot down a He 111 bomber and a Go 242 glider carrying 16 soldiers on Christmas day.

On 26 December, Galitski continued to attack with two divisions and 20 tanks, making his main push in the south and south-west. Fog and overcast skies prevented Luftwaffe air support. Although the defenders managed to destroy five tanks, another strongpoint, Preuss Berlin, was lost – its entire garrison was killed. Sensing that the defence was beginning to collapse, the Soviets kept attacking during the night, infiltrating through the ruins. The next morning, the Soviets mounted a major attack in the south and overran the Brünn, Nordlingen and Vienna strongpoints. In the south-west, Soviet tanks engaged the defenders of Stützpunkt Innsbruck at point-blank range, annihilating the entire garrison. Since most of their anti-tank guns were destroyed, the Germans were helpless against tank attacks. In order to hold onto the city centre, von Sass decided to abandon two positions in the eastern sector, Bromberg and Brandenberg, then ordered the troops to form a new line around the burnt-out wreckage of the train station. Both sides were completely exhausted, but Galitski could keep feeding fresh troops into the battle, such as the 100th Kazakh Rifle Brigade and even some march battalions made up of replacements.

The situation became even more critical for the defence on 28 December, as the Soviets began to push from the south and the north-west, to split the city in two. Despite overcast weather, the Luftwaffe managed to airdrop 13.8 tons of supplies. In order to provide some visible sign of support for the encircled garrison, Wöhler ordered his one long-range artillery battery – 2./schwere Artillerie-Abteilung 817, equipped with 17cm K18 guns (maximum range 22.7km) – to fire some missions against Soviet formations outside

A Soviet anti-tank squad waits in a village along the likely German axis of advance. The Soviet PTRD-41 anti-tank rifle lacked the ability to destroy enemy medium tanks, but it could inflict significant damage when multiple rifles fired against the same target. Soviet snipers also killed the commander of one Panzer battalion in the early days of the relief operation. (Author's collection)

A Ju 87 Stuka at a forward airstrip, near a pile of 250kg bombs. Due to winter weather conditions, the Stukas were not able to provide the quantity of close air support missions that army commanders desired to assist their ground operations. Furthermore, as the perimeter at Velikiye Luki shrank, the Stukas were used to deliver supply bombs to the encircled garrison. (Nik Cornish at www. Stavka.org.uk)

Velikiye Luki. During the night of 28/29 December, the Luftwaffe was able to land five gliders in Velikiye Luki and brought in two replacement 7.5cm anti-tank guns. Continued fair weather on 29 December allowed the Luftwaffe to deliver roughly 25 tons of supplies by glider and supply containers, which stiffened the defence. Soviet attacks in both the south and north-west were repulsed and von Sass evacuated the survivors from two exposed outposts in the south-east. About one-third of the garrison was now either dead, captured or wounded, leaving a hard core of resistance around the train station and marketplace in the centre and the Citadel in the west.

Around 0800hrs on 30 December, 249th Rifle Division began a major attack in the south-west corner of the city, near Stützpunkt Würzburg, using several battalions of infantry and KV-8 flame-thrower tanks. The flame-thrower tanks flushed out the defenders, blasting the enemy-held buildings at point-blank range; the German garrisons were annihilated. At the same time, 357th Rifle Division crossed the Lovat into the north-west corner of the city and began to roll up the supply troops assigned to defend this sector. In a matter of hours, the German defence along the Lovat collapsed and by mid-afternoon, only a narrow corridor connected the two halves of the German garrison. Von Sass ordered the remaining German troops in the western portion of the city to withdraw into the Citadel and Hauptmann Erich Darnedde, commander of I./Grenadier-Regiment 277, was put in charge of this group. By nightfall, the Soviets controlled everything on the west bank of the Lovat except the Citadel, which was now isolated. Von Sass retained command over the rest of the garrison from his bunker near the rail station. The Luftwaffe managed to deliver 5.3 tons of supplies to the increasingly small eastern perimeter, but the Citadel was on its own. A number of German units were surrounded as the Soviets bypassed their strongpoints, and during the night, these fragments tried to regain German lines. During the night of 30/31 December, a group of 28 soldiers – the remnants of three different companies – reached the Citadel.

Galitski kept up the pressure on 31 December, sending his tanks against the southern and eastern sectors. On this occasion, the garrison had received additional anti-tank guns and the defenders were able to successfully repulse the tanks, destroying five of them. However, between the near constant Soviet artillery fire and bombing raids, the defenders were forced to remain underground most of the time, in fetid basement shelters. The German wounded could not be evacuated and were succumbing to infection and malnutrition, while even the able-bodied soldiers were existing on a few hundred grams of bread per day. The inability of Gruppe Wöhler to make any advance in the past ten days also left the defenders with the feeling that they had been written off – morale was close to breaking point. Von Sass indicated that the garrison still had a combat strength of about 2,100 men, including about 500 in the Citadel; but over 2,000 were dead, wounded or missing. In fact, von Sass was probably guessing, since he had little contact with his remaining troops.

Meanwhile, Gruppe Wöhler spent two weeks regrouping and waiting for reinforcements, while von Sass' garrison was being decimated. Wöhler was left with the equivalent of about four combat-effective infantry battalions and about 30 armoured fighting vehicles. He adopted a by-the-book mindset, insisting that the relief operation should not be resumed until he had received a fresh division and another assault-gun battalion, plus decent weather for Luftwaffe support. Scherer was apoplectic that his division was being destroyed to so little purpose, but he had been sidelined since most of the remnants of his division had been pulled out of the line on 24 December – now he was just a spectator to disaster. Von der Chevallerie spent most of the time on the phone, pleading with von Kluge for additional forces, which only arrived piece-meal. Galitski was quick to notice that Gruppe Wöhler had halted, and he boldly decided to launch some local counter-attacks to keep the Germans off balance. The first attempt on 23 December, using Estonian troops from the 921st Rifle Regiment (249th Rifle Division), fell apart when hundreds of Estonian troops – including a battalion commander – deserted and fled to the Germans; German sources claim that over 700 Estonian troops defected, although prisoner records mention only 219 deserters in this period. Galitski responded to the Estonian mass desertions by relieving Saueselg, the commander of the 249th Rifle Division, and replacing him with an NKVD officer. Another attempt on 24 December, using 19th Rifle Division and some tanks, succeeded in evicting Grenadier-Regiment 76 from the village of Alekseikovo, one of the closest positions to Velikiye Luki. Oberst Paul Klatt, the indefatigable commander of Gebirgsjäger-Regiment 138, was also badly wounded on the same day, depriving Wöhler of a key tactical commander.

By this point, von Kluge was enough of a professional to recognize that it was highly unlikely that Gruppe Wöhler was going to reach Velikiye Luki in time. After the loss of Alekseikovo, von Kluge sent a request all the way to Hitler, requesting that von Sass' garrison be given the freedom of action to conduct an independent breakout operation. Hitler refused, just as he had refused one week earlier to grant Paulus' encircled 6.Armee at Stalingrad permission to break out. The defenders at Velikiye Luki would hold or die. Without authority to conduct a breakout and with no real reserves available, von Kluge, von der Chevallerie and Wöhler were left trying to cobble together a combat-effective force for one last attempt to reach Velikiye Luki before the garrison was annihilated. Von Kluge decided to transfer part of 331.Infanterie-Division from Spas-Demensk (under 4.Armee), part of 205.Infanterie-Division from Velizh (9.Armee) and a *Panzer-Abteilung* from 2.Panzer-Armee. These units had to be quietly pulled out of their current sectors, loaded onto trains and transported to Nevel, then marched about 40km along muddy backroads to assembly areas near Leshakovo. Only

German troops load supply containers beneath an He 111 bomber. The Luftwaffe used both He 111 bombers and Ju 87 dive-bombers to deliver these containers to the encircled garrison in Velikiye Luki. Sometimes they were dropped with parachutes, sometimes not. (Nik Cornish at www.Stavka.org.uk)

GLIDER DELIVERY, 0120HRS, 29 DECEMBER 1943 (PP. 68–69)

After the Soviet attacks on Christmas Day, the German garrison in Velikiye Luki was in dire condition and near collapse. The last anti-tank gun had been destroyed, and the garrison's artillery had nearly exhausted its ammunition. Gruppe Wöhler's relief effort was stalled in the snow, 9km south-west of Velikiye Luki. The Luftwaffe's efforts to fly more ammunition and weapons into the besieged city had been frustrated by miserable winter weather and Soviet anti-aircraft batteries on the outskirts. On Christmas morning, one Go 242 glider from 1.(Go)/VK(S) V tried to make it with 16 volunteers and supplies, but was shot down just short of the city. In desperation, Scherer demanded that the Luftwaffe make a superhuman effort to resupply his troops in Velikiye Luki, and von Greim agreed, irrespective of weather or losses. On the night of 28/29 December, five Go 242 gliders took off from Vitebsk, towed by He 111 bombers and headed for Velikiye Luki.

Around 0200hrs, the first gliders approached the city and were released from their tugs. The garrison had built a short runway for gliders near the eastern railway station in Velikiye Luki. A small Luftwaffe ground team used red and green lamps to mark the landing zone, although they had to conceal them as much as possible or the Soviets would fire upon the lights. Approaching the city through the dark winter murk, the glider pilots could not spot the lights until they were within 400m. Soviet machine-gunners opened fire on the silent gliders, but missed. Amazingly, five gliders successfully landed on the small ice runway before dawn, bringing vital ammunition, medical supplies and two 7.5cm anti-tank guns.

The scene shows one of the Go 242 gliders (**1**) that has landed. The landing zone is flat and ice-covered, and railway tracks lie off to the far side. Soldiers are unloading a 7.5cm anti-tank gun (**2**) and ammunition boxes from the back end of the glider, which has its hinged tail cone in raised position. A short ramp is deployed from the back of the glider. Nearby, a German soldier waits with two harnessed horses (**3**) to help pull the gun and ammunition away. In the foreground, a German Luftwaffe soldier (**4**) uses a hand-held lamp to mark the runway for the next glider. Soviet tracer fire (**5**) arcs into the air, trying to hit the next incoming glider.

Over the next two days, nine more gliders landed in Velikiye Luki. A few glider pilots were flown out in Fieseler Storch light planes so they could be recycled for additional glider sorties, but most joined the garrison. Thanks to the timely glider supply, Velikiye Luki's garrison was able to hold on for an additional two weeks.

a handful of reinforcements had reached Gruppe Wöhler by 31 December, which meant that the relief operation – designated as Operation *Totila* – kept getting pushed back.

Galitski continued to pound on Velikiye Luki's defenders in the first three days of January, slowly pushing von Sass' group into an ever-shrinking perimeter around the rail station. The main effort was made by 257th Rifle Division against Stützpunkt Kolberg in the northern part of the city and by 47th Mechanized Brigade against Stützpunkt

Nordlingen in the southern part of the city. Somehow, both positions were held, even though the combat strength of most of the German companies had been reduced to just 10–15 men. Only one 10.5cm howitzer was still operational, with a few rounds of ammunition. The 3rd Shock Army's assault units were also much reduced and most attacks were now battalion-size, supported by a few tanks. Dremov's 47th Mechanized Brigade continued to bite into the southern flank of the German perimeter, gradually working its way around German positions that could not be overrun.

The 2./Sanitäts-Kompanie 183 (medical company) was overwhelmed trying to deal with over 1,000 wounded and both of its doctors were dead or missing (one doctor was still working in the Citadel). The Luftwaffe tried to increase air supply drops, but frequent snowstorms made this difficult and Galitski had deployed two anti-aircraft regiments around the city. On 1 January, 11 He 111s were able to drop 9.7 tons of supplies to the garrison, but lost three aircraft to anti-aircraft fire. Hauptmann Darnedde's group at the Citadel was particularly difficult to supply, since the area it occupied was so tiny – most parachute containers fell into Russian hands. Given the difficulty of moving around in daylight, von Sass' troops usually recovered supply containers at night. Another 14 tons of supplies were dropped on 2 January, but very little over the next two days. On 3 January, Darnedde's group ran out of water and had eaten all of their horses. German morale was increasingly brittle as the prospect of defeat became closer. Von Sass reported to von der Chevallerie that he had been forced to summarily execute one of his *Landesschützen*, who had attempted to desert his post disguised in a Soviet uniform.

Listening to the increasingly grim radio reports from Velikiye Luki, von der Chevallerie realized that the end was near. Wöhler was methodically trying to build up a strong force for a full-scale attack and was willing to wait for the entire 331.Infanterie-Division to arrive, but this could take another week. The winter weather was also uncooperative, diminishing the probability of effective Luftwaffe support. Nevertheless, by the evening of 3 January, von der Chevallerie recognized that the garrison in Velikiye Luki could not hold out much longer and resolved to attack the next day no matter what; von Kluge concurred and authorized the operation to commence.

Aerial resupply was vital for keeping encircled German garrisons from collapsing, particularly ammunition. This canister includes hand grenades, which were consumed at a voracious rate in close-quarter city fighting. The 'supply bombs' (Abwurfbehälter für Nachschub) could carry up to 250kg of supplies, although rough landings often damaged the contents. Typically, a supply bomb carrying ammunition could hold 24 hand grenades or about 3,000 rounds of small-arms ammunition. (Süddeutsche Zeitung Bild 00384761, Foto: Scherl)

A German PzKpfw IV crew cleans the bore of their short-barrelled 7.5cm KwK 37 L/24 gun. It is extremely difficult to get tank crews to conduct field maintenance during severe winter conditions, when even touching frozen steel can result in lost skin or frostbite. The German steel tank tracks also had a tendency to freeze to icy ground overnight and could be difficult to move in the morning. (Nik Cornish at www. Stavka.org.uk)

OPERATION *TOTILA*, 4–14 JANUARY 1943

At 0830hrs on 4 January, Operation *Totila* began. Jaschke's division-size *Kampfgruppe* led the main effort on Gruppe Wöhler's right with Grenadier-Regiment 76, two battalions from 205.Infanterie-Division (III./Grenadier-Regiment 335 and II./Grenadier-Regiment 358), Jäger-Bataillon 3, I./Panzer-Regiment 15 (21 tanks) and 11 assault guns. On Wöhler's left flank, Göritz's 291.Infanterie-Division attacked with two battalion-size *Kampfgruppen* from his own division (Grenadier-Regiment 504, Grenadier-Regiment 505), two battalions from 331.Infanterie-Division (II./Grenadier-Regiment 558 and I./Grenadier-Regiment 559), Panzer-Abteilung 18 (22 tanks) and ten assault guns. Wöhler kept Jäger-Bataillon 5 and Jäger-Bataillon 6 and 8./Panzer-Regiment 29 (17 tanks) in reserve. Gruppe Wöhler had assembled 12 heavy and 60 light howitzers to support the attack, as well as 36 Nebelwerfer. Operation *Totila* was designed as a single-axis offensive, with the two division spearheads advancing side by side; only burnt-out units were left to protect the flanks, as Gruppe Wöhler advanced. Von der Chevallerie ordered Brandenberger's 8.Panzer-Division to assist the operation with diversionary attacks to tie down at least some Soviet units in their sector. Jaschke's formation got off to a good start, first recovering the village of Alekseikovo then sprinting forwards nearly 2km to seize Ivansevo. Göritz's column had more difficulty breaching the Soviet defences on Hill 180.9 and at Kolyuki, and his troops suffered enfilading from Soviet artillery deployed to the west. Baranov's 19th Guards Rifle Division put up a tough fight, but was unable to hold. Eventually, Göritz was able to break through and advance about 1km to Sakhny, forcing Baranov's division back a bit.

Rather than simply wait for the Germans to resume their advance on 5 January, Galitski conducted a strong spoiling attack against Göritz's column at dawn, using artillery and Il-2 Sturmovik attacks to strike German troop concentrations. In spite of this bombardment, Gruppe Wöhler continued to methodically advance another kilometre and spent the day clearing Soviet

Operation *Totila*, 4–10 January 1943

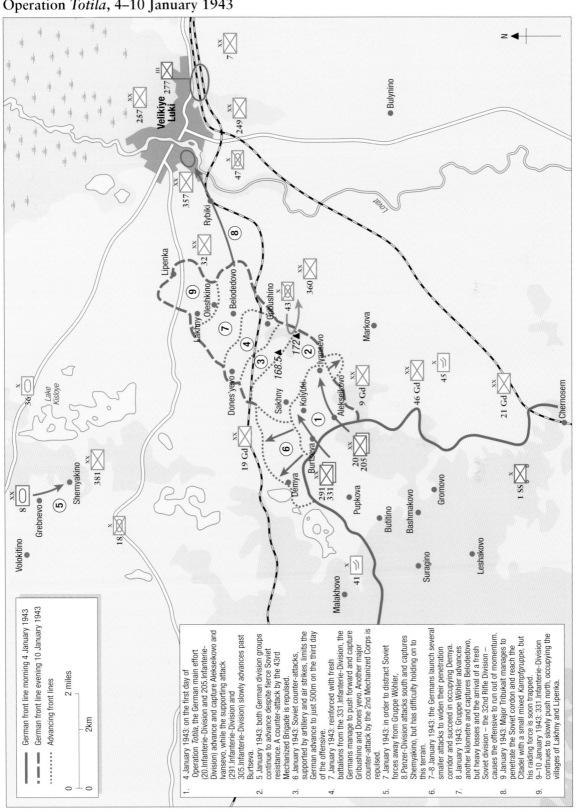

1. 4 January 1943: on the first day of Operation *Totila*, the German main effort (20.Infanterie-Division and 205.Infanterie-Division) advance and capture Alekseikovo and Ivansevo, while the supporting attack (291.Infanterie-Division and 305.Infanterie-Division) slowly advances past Burtseva.

2. 5 January 1943: both German division groups continue to advance despite fierce Soviet resistance. A counter-attack by the 43rd Mechanized Brigade is repulsed.

3. 6 January 1943: Soviet counter-attacks, supported by artillery and air strikes, limits the German advance to just 500m on the third day of the offensive.

4. 7 January 1943: reinforced with fresh battalions from the 331.Infanterie-Division, the Germans manage to push forward and capture Gribushino and Dones'yevo. Another major counter-attack by the 2nd Mechanized Corps is repulsed.

5. 7 January 1943: in order to distract Soviet forces away from Gruppe Wöhler, 8.Panzer-Division attacks south and captures Shemyakino, but has difficulty holding on to this terrain.

6. 7–8 January 1943: the Germans launch several smaller attacks to widen their penetration corridor and succeed in occupying Demya.

7. 8 January 1943: Gruppe Wöhler advances another kilometre and captures Belodedovo, but heavy losses and the arrival of a fresh Soviet division – the 32nd Rifle Division – causes the offensive to run out of momentum.

8. 9 January 1943: Major Tribukait manages to penetrate the Soviet cordon and reach the Citadel with a small mixed *Kampfgruppe*, but his raiding force is soon trapped.

9. 9–10 January 1943: 331.Infanterie-Division continues to slowly push north, occupying the villages of Lakhny and Lipenka.

73

A Soviet light machine-gunner within the ruins of Velikiye Luki. The Soviets had to methodically clear out each building, which was time-consuming, and the defenders were sometimes able to recapture buildings with well-timed counterattacks. (Author's collection)

resistance from two hilltops in its path – Hill 168.5 and Hill 172.0. Korchagin's 2nd Mechanized Corps committed its 43rd Mechanized Brigade to contest these hills in a series of counter-attacks. The Germans destroyed nine Soviet tanks, but their progress was reduced to a glacial pace. Once again, Galitski pre-empted Wöhler's attack and hit the German relief force hard with his artillery and air strikes from 3rd Air Army on the morning of 6 January. One German assault gun was set on fire after being strafed by an Il-2 Sturmovik, while another was flipped over by near misses from artillery fire. The Luftwaffe responded with multiple fighter sorties from III./Jagdgeschwader 54, which claimed 14 kills for the loss of one Bf-109G fighter. Feldwebel Kurt Ströber of 7./Jagdgeschwader 54, who had served with the Legion Condor in Spain, had a particularly good day, claiming five victories in three sorties. Yet the Soviet air and artillery attacks disrupted Gruppe Wöhler enough so that no real progress was made on the ground on 6 January. The only good news for Wöhler was that more of Generalmajor Franz Beyer's 331.Infanterie-Division had now arrived and was ready to join the operation.

A strong frost occurred during the night of 6/7 January, with temperatures dropping to -12° C (10° F). Wöhler intended that Beyer's fresh division would lead the advance on the morning of 7 January, but this unit was slow to reach the front and instead Jaschke's formation continued to spearhead the attack. Rather than advance north-east directly towards Velikiye Luki, Jaschke shifted north to Gribushino, which apparently surprised Galitski. Jaschke's troops crossed the Novosokolniki–Velikiye Luki rail line and led by several battalions from 205.Infanterie-Division, they managed to capture Gribushino, just 6km from the Citadel. Stukas from Sturzkampfgeschwader 77 assisted the attack with precision dive-bombing on Soviet positions. Beyer's troops finally got into the fight during the afternoon and advanced to the left of Jaschke's formation, capturing the village of Dones'yevo. Counter-attacks by 2nd Mechanized Corps were repulsed, with 13 Soviet tanks destroyed. Under pressure to assist Gruppe Wöhler, Brandenberger's 8.Panzer-Division mounted an attack west of Lake Kisloye with a mixed *Kampfgruppe* led by Major Walter Menningen. Initially, the attack achieved surprise and culminated in a 3km advance that overran a Soviet 122mm artillery battery in Shemyakino. However, Major Menningen lacked the troops to hold this terrain, and the Soviets responded with dense artillery barrages and counter-attacks that forced the *Kampfgruppe* to pull back the next day. During the enemy counter-attacks, the commander of I./Panzer-Regiment 10 was killed and one of the division's few PzKpfw III tanks was destroyed.

Concerned that Gruppe Wöhler might actually reach Velikiye Luki, Galitski committed a fresh division – Polkovnik Ivan S. Bezugly's 32nd Rifle Division – to reinforce the western approaches to the city. Wöhler's progress noticeably slowed on 8 January, although 331.Infanterie-Division was able to capture the villages of Belodedovo and Oleshkino, 5km west of the city.

Meanwhile, reports from Velikiye Luki were growing worse by the day. On 5 January, Soviet tanks broke through near the railway station and destroyed the last howitzers. The glider landing zone was also overrun, and it was now almost impossible for the Luftwaffe to accurately parachute supplies to the remaining German-held areas, which consisted of indistinguishable ruined buildings. Von Sass melodramatically radioed: 'we are fighting to the last man and the last cartridge'. On 6 January, Dremov's 47th Mechanized Brigade made another major push against Stützpunkt Vienna, supported by the armoured flame-throwers of 515th Flame-thrower Tank Battalion; the Germans destroyed three tanks but lost two more precious anti-tank guns. Another new 7.5cm anti-tank gun and crew was brought in by glider. On 7 January, 917th Rifle Regiment (7th Rifle Division) began clearing out the ruined railway station, eliminating the Germans on one floor, then the next. Only small numbers of Germans were captured. Several cores of resistance remained in the east–central section of Velikiye Luki, but von Sass no longer had a perimeter and Soviet troops were infiltrating into the city from every direction. On 8 January, Soviet flame-thrower tanks led the 249th Rifle Division's advance into the city centre, destroying three anti-tank guns and overrunning Stützpunkt Berlin II. The German defenders were now virtually defenceless and running out of ammunition. Gruppe Wöhler fired long-range artillery missions to support the garrison, but most of its observers had already been used up fighting as infantrymen. Stukas from III./Sturzkampfgeschwader 77 also managed to bomb some Soviet targets around Velikiye Luki, but could not inflict enough damage to make a real difference.

Von Kluge arrived at Wöhler's command post on the morning of 9 January to see for himself how Operation *Totila* was progressing. Losses from enemy artillery barrages and counter-attacks were quickly wearing down the relief force to the point that most units would soon be combat ineffective. The I./Panzer-Regiment 15 had lost 18 of its 21 tanks and the

Soviet infantry advance in small groups along the streets of Velikiye Luki. Note how each building is badly damaged by artillery and small-arms fire. The Germans typically held the lower levels of buildings, which afforded maximum protection from Soviet artillery. (Author's collection)

MAJOR TRIBUKAIT'S DASH, 1530HRS, 9 JANUARY 1943 (PP. 76–77)

By 8 January 1943, the German relief operation had ground to a halt 5km west of Velikiye Luki, stopped by deep snow and intense Soviet resistance. Gruppe Wöhler could not reach Velikiye Luki and the garrison could not survive for much longer. In desperation, Major Günther Tribukait, commander of Jäger-Battalion 5, volunteered to lead a raiding force to reach the Citadel and then help the garrison to mount a breakout operation. In addition to 83 men from his battalion mounted on eight SdKfz 251 Schützenpanzerwagen and one SdKfz 10/4 (2cm Flak) half-track, Tribukait was provided with eight tanks (three PzKpfw III and five PzKpfw IV) from I./Panzer-Regiment 15 and one StuG III assault gun. On the afternoon of 9 January, Major Tribukait assembled his raiding force near the village of Belodedovo and instructed his crews to 'keep moving and firing', and that they were to stop for nothing. Disabled vehicles would be abandoned. Normally, German mechanized units advanced methodically, but in this case Major Tribukait proposed to charge through the Soviet lines at maximum speed, hoping to catch the enemy by surprise. It was a bold, but highly desperate gamble.

Around 1400hrs, Major Tribukait's vehicles moved out through the German forward lines at high speed. Initially, they had to cross a large, frozen open moor, but the lack of a preparatory artillery barrage caught the Soviets by surprise. The German vehicles advanced in a tight wedge, with the tanks in front, shooting at any Soviets in their immediate path. Once the Soviet defenders realized what was occurring, they opened fire from all sides, with anti-tank guns and machine guns.

In this scene, Major Tribukait and his half-track are shown at lower right (1), as the Germans speed towards the smoking ruins of Velikiye Luki some 4km distant (2). A wedge of several German tanks (3) is advancing in front of his SPW, with guns facing to the left, front and right. Tribukait's SPW is passing a destroyed Soviet 45mm anti-tank gun position (4), which has been run over by a German tank. Soldiers in his half-track are firing at Soviet infantry in the woods (5). One German SdKfz 251 has been hit up ahead (6), and is burning furiously.

Amazingly, Tribukait's column punched through the Soviet lines and reached the Citadel at 1506hrs, to the great joy of the trapped garrison. However, the Soviets immediately called in heavy artillery fire on the Citadel, which gradually battered the armoured vehicles into wrecks. A lucky hit on a PzKpfw III tank blocked the main entrance to the Citadel. Furthermore, Tribukait's vehicles were nearly out of fuel and ammunition, with no hope of resupply. Major Tribukait would lead the breakout from Velikiye Luki on the night of 15/16 January, but on foot.

A 203mm howitzer M1931. Stavka had withdrawn these heavy artillery pieces from front-line service due to heavy losses in 1941, but they returned to action with the Soviet winter counter-offensive in November 1942. At least one battery of these heavy howitzers began shelling Velikiye Luki on 18 December 1942. (Nik Cornish at www. Stavka.org.uk)

lead battalions of 205.Infanterie-Division had lost most of their company commanders in the first two days of fighting. Likewise, the three assault battalions from 331.Infanterie-Division had been reduced to between only 60 and 120 effectives each. In particular, von Kluge noted that the troops of 331.Infanterie-Division, who had been manning a quiet sector of the front, were unprepared for mobile warfare and were dying like flies due to inadequate training. It was the relentless pounding from the Soviet artillery that was bleeding Gruppe Wöhler dry; German infantrymen could not dig into the frozen soil and were particularly vulnerable to Katyusha rocket barrages. Von Kluge visited several other tactical command posts and saw that the relief operation was grinding to a halt. It is unclear if von Kluge suggested the next move or whether it came from below, but it was clearly time for one last desperate throw of the dice. Major Günther Tribukait, commander of Jäger-Battalion 5, volunteered to lead a raiding force with 83 of his Jägers and some of the remaining tanks to reach the Citadel and then help the garrison to mount a breakout operation. It is also unclear who approved this radical approach, but Tribukait was provided with most of the remaining combat-effective armoured fighting vehicles: eight tanks (three PzKpfw III and five PzKpfw IV), one assault gun and nine half-tracks to carry his raiding force. Apparently, no effort was made to check the fuel and ammunition status on these vehicles, which was actually quite low.

Tribukait's raiding party assembled in a gully west of Belodedovo and jumped off just before 1400hrs. The Soviet troops in the area were caught completely by surprise, since there was no artillery preparation and the German vehicles simply advanced at maximum speed towards Soviet positions, firing and moving. Most of the column easily penetrated the thin front-line Soviet positions, but one PzKpfw III was hit by anti-tank fire and disabled. Gefreiter Werner Bürkner and another crewman made it out of the burning wreck and were picked up by a passing SPW, but this vehicle was also soon disabled by enemy fire. Bürkner and some of the Jägers were captured and he witnessed a Soviet officer execute seven of them on the spot, before

A KV-8 flame-thrower tank. Galitski was provided with a battalion of KV-8 flame-thrower tanks to spearhead the assault into Velikiye Luki, and they proved extremely useful in eliminating German strongpoints. Due to their thick armour, the lighter German 3.7cm Pak anti-tank gun was useless against the KV-8, and even the 5cm gun had difficulty against this beast. (Author's collection)

the survivors were led to the rear. Meanwhile, Tribukait somehow managed to reach the Citadel with the bulk of his column intact, which caused an outburst of joy from Hauptmann Darnedde's survivors. However, the Soviets recovered from their initial surprise and responded to the bold German raid with heavy artillery fire directed against the Citadel. In order to seek cover, Tribukait decided to drive his column through one of the Citadel's narrow gates and shelter within its walls, but the last tank received a direct hit, which disabled it, blocking the gateway. Tribukait's column was now trapped inside the Citadel. Soviet artillery pounded the interior of the Citadel, knocking out five of the seven tanks and four of the seven SPWs. Yet even if the column had not been trapped inside the Citadel, the vehicles had fired most of their ammunition on the way in and were also almost out of fuel; this is the kind of situation that can occur when a light infantryman is put in charge of tanks. Tribukait also falsely assumed that the Luftwaffe could airdrop more fuel and ammunition for his armoured vehicles into the Citadel, but he soon discovered this was impossible. Instead, Tribukait now assumed command of the 509-man garrison in the Citadel, having shot his bolt.

Galitski immediately placed blocking forces to prevent any more German forces from following Tribukait. From this point on, Galitski used his superiority in artillery and tanks to keep Gruppe Wöhler off balance. Gromov's 3rd Air Army also mounted continuous ground-attack sorties, which severely rattled the Germans. Unable to follow Tribukait's path, Gruppe Wöhler tried to shift northwards to Lakhny, but made only minor gains on 10 January. Inside Velikiye Luki, the Soviets finally overran the train station and brought von Sass' command bunker under direct fire. Stukas from Sturzkampfgeschwader 77 dropped some supply bombs, but only three were recovered by German troops. On 11 January, the Soviets overran Stützpunkt Budapest in the south-east, and now the Germans only held a few islands of resistance in the eastern part of the city. Stützpunkt Braunschweig, in the north-east, used the last operational 7.5cm leichtes IG18 to destroy two light tanks, but the gun was also destroyed. In the Citadel, the last of Major Tribukait's armoured fighting vehicles were destroyed by enemy artillery fire.

Operation *Totila* had culminated short of its objective, but Gruppe Wöhler continued to make futile efforts to reach the Citadel. On 11 January, 205.Infanterie-Division sent Kampfgruppe Ramdohr to try to advance east from Lakhny to Fotneva, but the Soviets shot this group to pieces. Another attempt on 12 and 13 January to reach the Citadel with Kampfgruppe Borho (I./Grenadier-Regiment 353 and Jäger-Bataillon 3) through Rybiki managed to gain a little ground, but was halted 2,200m south-west of the Citadel – this was Gruppe Wöhler's high-water mark. Having exhausted all the available infantry formations, Wöhler appealed for more reinforcements, and

Reichsmarschall Göring finally agreed to release one battalion of 7.Flieger-Division to lead another attempt to reach the Citadel – a futile gesture, at best. However, Hauptmann Karl-Heinz Becker's III./Fallschirmjäger-Regiment 1 did not reach Belodedovo until the night of 15/16 January, and last-minute haggling about its role left it in limbo. Wöhler wanted the battalion, along with a few assault guns, to try to reach the Citadel in a night attack, but Becker was reluctant to mount what looked like a suicide mission. Instead, Becker's battalion was placed in a tactical assembly area, where it was subjected to enemy artillery and air attacks for a full day, then put in the line to defend a forward position north-east of Gribushino. The Fallschirmjägers faced repeated enemy ground attacks on 16 and 17 January, incurring heavy losses – including Becker and two company commanders, who were wounded – for no purpose. Altogether, III./Fallschirmjäger-Regiment 1 started with a strength of 475 troops and suffered 47 dead, 25 missing and 244 wounded (66 per cent losses) in just a few days of defensive combat. Finally, the battalion was withdrawn on the night of 19/20 January, having been reduced to just 159 effectives. Operation *Totila* had failed.

THE END AT VELIKIYE LUKI, 13–17 JANUARY 1943

As Operation *Totila* sputtered out, the Soviets set about exterminating the last German positions in eastern Velikiye Luki. Stützpunkt Vienna was overrun on 13 January and von Sass was surrounded in his command bunker. The Luftwaffe continued with its daily airdrops, but most fell into enemy hands now or were unrecoverable in no-man's-land. The defenders still had a little food left – about 85g of meat and 250g of bread per man per day – but since the Luftwaffe could no longer reliably deliver supplies by air, this hand-to-mouth existence could not last long. Major Tribukait reported that German observers in the Citadel could see Soviet tanks crossing the railway bridge into the city, but he could do nothing to interfere. Kronik's 357th Rifle Division mounted a regimental-size attack against the Citadel, and even managed to get troops atop its ramparts before being repulsed. Two Soviet tanks that penetrated into the inner courtyard of the Citadel were destroyed by German grenadiers in close combat. Chagrined by this setback, Kronik pulled back his troops and resorted to siege tactics, relying upon artillery and starvation to weaken the garrison before another assault. However, Tribukait and Darnedde had barely enough men to man the parapets, and they were only surviving on a few aerial resupply canisters per day.

On the afternoon of 15 January, Gruppe Wöhler radioed both Tribukait in the Citadel and von Sass near the railway station and informed them that they

A 21cm Mörser 18 from 2.Mörser-Batterie, Artillerie-Regiment 736 lies abandoned in Velikiye Luki after the battle. The Germans based their defence of Velikiye Luki on the idea that the garrison would have plenty of fire support, unlike Kholm in early 1942. While the provision of heavy artillery enabled the garrison to fend off the early Soviet attacks, it proved impossible to deliver ammunition for heavy artillery by parachute drops. (Author's collection)

FINAL EFFORTS TO RELIEVE VELIKIYE LUKI, 11–16 JANUARY 1943

By 11 January 1943, it was clear Gruppe Wöhler lacked the strength to reach Velikiye Luki before the annihilation of the encircled garrison. Nevertheless, the Germans made several desperate attempts to reach the city, while the remaining defenders in the Citadel prepared to attempt a breakout.

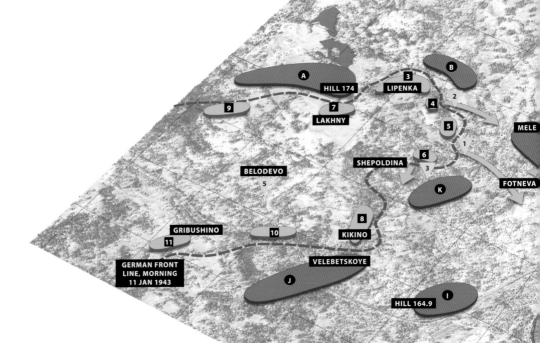

▼ EVENTS

1. 12 January: Grenadier-Regiment 335 from 205.Infanterie-Division finally captures the village of Fotneva after three days of fighting. Some scouts reach the outskirts of Rybiki, but cannot hold the terrain.

2. 12–13 January: Elements of 331.Infanterie-Division attempt to capture Melenka, but are stopped by intense fire. Eventually, this *Kampfgruppe* must withdraw.

3. 13 January: Elements of Grenadier-Regiment 335 capture Shepoldina, but are stopped by Soviet barrage fire.

4. 15 January, morning: The Soviet 357th Rifle Division attacks the Citadel with a reinforced regiment and tanks, and briefly penetrates the German defence before being repulsed.

5. 15 January: The Fallschirmjäger of III/.Fallschirmjäger-Regiment 1 are assembled near Belodedovo to spearhead a push towards Rybiki, but the effort is aborted and instead, the battalion is used to repel Soviet counter-attacks near Gribushino.

6. 16 January, 0200hrs: The German breakout from the Citadel begins, led by Major Tribukait. His group fights their way through several Soviet positions, and reaches German lines near Melenka with 102 soldiers around 0530hrs.

7. 16 January, 1600hrs: Von Sass and most of the remaining German garrison surrenders.

205   SEYFFARDT

331   BEYER

Note: gridlines are shown at intervals of 1km (0.62 miles)

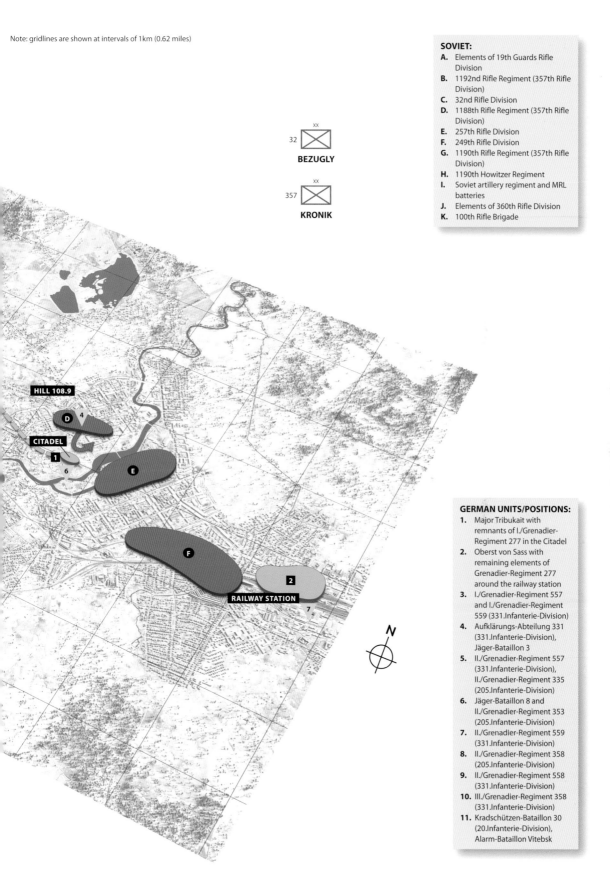

BEZUGLY

KRONIK

SOVIET:

A. Elements of 19th Guards Rifle Division
B. 1192nd Rifle Regiment (357th Rifle Division)
C. 32nd Rifle Division
D. 1188th Rifle Regiment (357th Rifle Division)
E. 257th Rifle Division
F. 249th Rifle Division
G. 1190th Rifle Regiment (357th Rifle Division)
H. 1190th Howitzer Regiment
I. Soviet artillery regiment and MRL batteries
J. Elements of 360th Rifle Division
K. 100th Rifle Brigade

HILL 108.9

CITADEL

RAILWAY STATION

GERMAN UNITS/POSITIONS:

1. Major Tribukait with remnants of I./Grenadier-Regiment 277 in the Citadel
2. Oberst von Sass with remaining elements of Grenadier-Regiment 277 around the railway station
3. I./Grenadier-Regiment 557 and I./Grenadier-Regiment 559 (331.Infanterie-Division)
4. Aufklärungs-Abteilung 331 (331.Infanterie-Division), Jäger-Bataillon 3
5. II./Grenadier-Regiment 557 (331.Infanterie-Division), II./Grenadier-Regiment 335 (205.Infanterie-Division)
6. Jäger-Bataillon 8 and II./Grenadier-Regiment 353 (205.Infanterie-Division)
7. II./Grenadier-Regiment 559 (331.Infanterie-Division)
8. II./Grenadier-Regiment 358 (205.Infanterie-Division)
9. II./Grenadier-Regiment 558 (331.Infanterie-Division)
10. III./Grenadier-Regiment 358 (331.Infanterie-Division)
11. Kradschützen-Bataillon 30 (20.Infanterie-Division), Alarm-Bataillon Vitebsk

Two of Major Tribukait's tanks lie knocked out in the ruins near the Citadel. Note the Winterketten extended tracks on the PzKpfw III tank in the foreground. All of the tanks that reached the Citadel were lost. (Author's collection)

had been granted permission to attempt a breakout on their own. Both officers were told that one more relief effort was going to be made by the Fallschirmjäger battalion, but by this point few believed that Gruppe Wöhler would arrive in time. Von Sass reported that he could not attempt a breakout because too many of his men were wounded, but Tribukait decided to launch a breakout while there was still a chance. On the evening of 15 January, Tribukait, Darnedde and the other remaining officers developed a breakout plan, but opted not to inform the 200 wounded men in the Citadel – they would be left behind. The two surviving medical officers opted to remain with the wounded. At 0200hrs on 16 January, after the moon had set, Tribukait began the breakout. The Germans silently crept out of the main gate of the Citadel into the darkness, moving single file in squad-size groups, with intervals of several minutes between groups. Kronik's troops had pulled back a bit from the Citadel because they didn't want to get hit by their own artillery, which left a cratered no-man's-land outside. At first, the Soviets did not notice the breakout, and the groups that left first were able to infiltrate through some of the outposts, quietly killing sentries with knives. However, the Soviets finally noticed something and started sending up flares, illuminating the groups that were still in the open. Once the firing began, some of the German wounded realized that they were being left behind and some decided to try and escape as well. In a series of chaotic small-unit night actions, the groups led by Tribukait and Darnedde managed to fight their way through the Soviet ring and reach the forward positions held by 331.Infanterie-Division around 0530hrs. Tribukait brought out 102 survivors with him, and even a handful of the walking wounded came in soon afterwards. Altogether, 182 soldiers from the Citadel succeeded in reaching German lines. After sunrise, soldiers from Kronik's 357th Rifle Division moved into the silent Citadel and captured the remaining 235 German personnel.

In the eastern section of Velikiye Luki, von Sass sent his last radio messages to Gruppe Wöhler on the morning of 15 January. The Soviets were using 76mm guns firing point-blank to eliminate one German bunker after

Another view of abandoned German PzKpfw IV and PzKpfw III tanks near the Citadel in Velikiye Luki. Although all the tanks were damaged by Soviet artillery fire, it was the failure to ensure fuel and ammunition resupply that doomed the Panzer column to entombment within the city. (Author's collection)

another. Bunkers that continued to resist were blown up with satchel charges or burned by flame-thrower tanks. Finally, the Soviets informed von Sass that his bunker would be blown up unless he surrendered. At 1600hrs on 16 January, von Sass and his staff surrendered to troops from the Estonian 917th Rifle Regiment. A few minor German strongpoints held out for another 24 hours, before they too were eliminated. Only four German soldiers from the eastern section of Velikiye Luki reached German lines, one of whom was Oberleutnant Behnemann, a battery commander from Artillerie-Regiment 183. Behnemann's bunker near the railway station had been overrun by Soviet tanks and troops on the morning of 14 January, but he was able to hide and avoid capture. Setting out on his own, Oberleutnant Behnemann moved through the ruins during hours of darkness and managed to pass through multiple Soviet positions before reaching open woodland north-west of the city. After marching 40km, Behnemann managed to reach the forward positions of 8.Panzer-Division on 17 January.

The Soviets claimed to have captured 3,944 Germans in the Velikiye Luki operation, plus another 344 from forces outside the pocket. However, only 11 members of the Velikiye Luki garrison returned to Germany from Soviet captivity after the war, which suggests an unusually high attrition rate of around 99.5 per cent. Accounts from the few survivors such as Oberleutnant Behnemann mention that he saw a column of about 500–600 German prisoners in the eastern portion of the city, but he does not mention any wounded. Other German anecdotal accounts suggest that many of the wounded were left to freeze to death and that there were plenty of summary executions of prisoners in the final days of the siege. Given that there is no Soviet photographic evidence of a large prisoner haul at Velikiye Luki – as there was at Stalingrad a few weeks later – it appears that very few members of the German garrison survived the initial moments of captivity. Indeed, the available evidence – fragmentary as it is – suggests that major war crimes were committed by the Red Army in the hour of victory at Velikiye Luki. Having spurned surrender, most of von Sass' troops were apparently either summarily executed or left to freeze to death.

Strategic situation, 25 March 1943

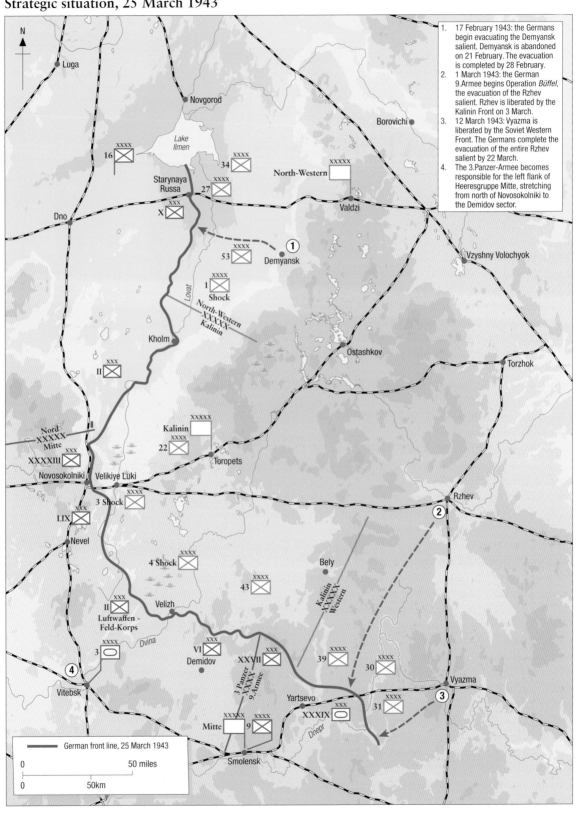

1. 17 February 1943: the Germans begin evacuating the Demyansk salient. Demyansk is abandoned on 21 February. The evacuation is completed by 28 February.
2. 1 March 1943: the German 9.Armee begins Operation *Büffel*, the evacuation of the Rzhev salient. Rzhev is liberated by the Kalinin Front on 3 March.
3. 12 March 1943: Vyazma is liberated by the Soviet Western Front. The Germans complete the evacuation of the entire Rzhev salient by 22 March.
4. The 3.Panzer-Armee becomes responsible for the left flank of Heeresgruppe Mitte, stretching from north of Novosokolniki to the Demidov sector.

German front line, 25 March 1943

0 ————— 50 miles

0 ————— 50km

AFTERMATH

Despite achieving operational success by capturing Velikiye Luki and eliminating the German garrison, Stavka viewed the operation in more critical terms because of crippling losses that prevented the 3rd Shock Army from seizing any additional objectives, such as Novosokolniki. Indeed, Velikiye Luki looked like a Pyrrhic victory. Given Purkayev's earlier failure to capture Kholm and his front's concurrent defeat in Operation *Mars*, Purkayev was the obvious choice as a scapegoat for the Red Army's operational failures. Three months after the liberation of Velikiye Luki, Purkayev was relieved and transferred to Siberia to command the Far Eastern Front for the rest of the war. Galitski remained in command of the 3rd Shock Army long

A Soviet T-34 tank and troops in the wreckage of Velikiye Luki after the German surrender. At great cost, the Red Army had conquered a ruined, lifeless city in the midst of a frozen wasteland. (Author's collection)

enough to see it finally capture Nevel in October 1943; he was then shifted to command the 11th Guards Army, which spearheaded the drive into East Prussia in 1945. Both Beloborodov and Korchagin remained as successful tactical commanders for the rest of the war. The 3rd Shock Army helped lead the push into the Baltic States in 1944 and ended the war in Berlin.

On the German side, the Velikiye Luki campaign was regarded as an unmitigated disaster, but was quickly overshadowed by the even larger catastrophe at Stalingrad. A few heroes emerged from Velikiye Luki: Major Tribukait and Hauptmann Darnedde were both awarded the Ritterkreuz des Eisernen Kreuzes for their role in leading the breakout. Tribukait continued to be a lucky individual throughout the war, but afterwards he was tried for war crimes in Yugoslavia and executed in 1947. Von der Chevallerie played a major role in the breakout of Hube's 1.Panzer-Armee in 1944 but he fell out of favour with Hitler and was placed in reserve; he died during the Soviet invasion of Pomerania in 1945. Otto Wöhler rose to command a corps, then an army, then an army group in the last two years of the war, although his relief operation to save encircled German forces in the Cherkassy pocket in 1944 was a notable failure. After the war, Wöhler was convicted of complicity in war crimes by the Allies and spent three years in prison. Scherer remained in command of the shattered 83.Infanterie-Division until March 1944, then spent the remainder of the war in staff roles, for which he was unsuited.

Due to the catastrophe at Stalingrad and the loss of Velikiye Luki, OKH finally succeeded in convincing Hitler that holding onto vulnerable positions such as Demyansk and Rzhev was wasteful of resources. On 31 January 1943, Hitler finally authorized the evacuation of both salients. On 17 February, Heeresgruppe Nord began Operation *Ziethen* and successfully evacuated all forces from the Demyansk salient by the end of the month. Heeresgruppe Mitte successfully evacuated the Rzhev salient with Operation *Büffel*, which was completed by March. The evacuation of both salients greatly reduced the German front line and actually created a surplus of units that could be used to create a mobile reserve to deal with future Soviet offensives. However, Hitler refused to countenance using these reserves for purely defensive purposes, and immediately began thinking of ways to use them for a counter-offensive in the summer of 1943. The Velikiye Luki–Nevel–Novosokolniki sector remained just as vulnerable throughout 1943 as it was before the Soviet winter offensive. Indeed, once the Kalinin Front occupied Velikiye Luki, the Red Army was in a good position to push towards Vitebsk in the summer of 1943, yet OKH completely stripped this sector of reserves in order to mount the offensive at Kursk.

Meanwhile, von Sass and the rest of the German officer prisoners were sent to NKVD Camp 160 located in Suzdal, 190km east of Moscow. In January 1946, von Sass was transported back to Velikiye Luki, along with a number of other German prisoners from the garrison for a show trial. Generalleutnant Fritz Georg von Rappard, the former commander of Grenadier-Regiment 277, who had been captured in 1945, was also brought to Velikiye Luki. On 31 January, a Soviet military tribunal found von Sass, von Rappard, Major Wilhelm Sonnewald (the *Ortskommandant* – town commander), Hauptmann Walter Knauf and four enlisted soldiers guilty of crimes against the population of Velikiye Luki and sentenced them to death. The eight condemned prisoners were then brought to the market

place in Velikiye Luki on 1 February 1946 and hanged in front of the entire town's population. The bodies were left hanging for three days, then buried in unmarked graves somewhere along the Nevel–Novosokolniki road. The Soviet treatment of von Sass and von Rappard, as well as other captives from Velikiye Luki, suggest retribution for a tenacious defence that cost the Red Army dearly, rather than any connection to specific war crimes. While the liberation of Velikiye Luki was a significant operational-level victory for the Red Army, the subsequent treatment of the defeated German garrison was disgraceful.

German prisoners marching out of Velikiye Luki, January 1943. The Red Army claimed to have captured nearly 4,000 troops at Velikiye Luki but unlike Stalingrad, there is little anecdotal or photographic evidence to support this claim. This column has roughly 200 prisoners and only a handful of guards. Based on German eyewitness accounts and the very small number of survivors repatriated after the war, it seems that very few members of the German garrison made it to POW camps. Note that none of the prisoners appear to be wounded. (Author's collection)

ANALYSIS

The loss of virtually the entire garrison of Velikiye Luki was a psychological shock to the Wehrmacht, since it was the first significant German formation to be annihilated in World War II. Just two weeks later, over 90,000 German troops from 6.Armee surrendered at Stalingrad. Velikiye Luki and Stalingrad proved to be two significant signposts on the Third Reich's path to defeat. The reasons for operational failure were not difficult to discern. The Wehrmacht had been designed to conduct short, sharp manoeuvre campaigns (*Bewegungskrieg*) with complete units in moderate terrain and weather conditions, which proved ill-suited to conducting ad hoc relief

Oberst von Sass in Soviet captivity. Although von Sass had not been linked to any war crimes in Russia, he was hanged after a post-war show trial in Velikiye Luki, along with seven other survivors. According to some Soviet anecdotal accounts, the prisoners were made to beg for their lives in the courtroom – which was then refused. The Soviet operational triumph at Velikiye Luki was tarnished by a display of medieval-style cruelty, which had to later be swept under the rug. (Author's collection)

operations with fragments of burnt-out divisions in the frozen marshes around Velikiye Luki. Not only were all the German units involved in the campaign significantly understrength in terms of manpower and equipment, but they also came from different commands and had not previously worked together – which seriously undermined unit cohesion. Close air support was also an integral element of *Bewegungskrieg*, but the frequent periods of rain and snowy weather made it extremely difficult for the Luftwaffe to support either the relief forces or the encircled garrison. Since manoeuvre was impossible, the relief forces relied upon brute force to reach their objective, but this battle of attrition only bled the already reduced units white. Unlike the Stalingrad relief operation, *Wintergewitter*, the effort to relieve Velikiye Luki lasted much longer and came much closer to its goal, but still failed. In addition to the 6,700 troops killed or captured in Velikiye Luki, Gruppe Chevallerie suffered about 20,000 casualties during the campaign, including over 5,000 dead or missing. Altogether, six German divisions were effectively gutted during the campaign and had to be pulled out of the line to refit. The Luftwaffe also suffered heavy losses during the Velikiye Luki campaign, including 17 He 111s shot down. Aerial resupply drops over Velikiye Luki resulted in a 4 per cent loss rate to enemy Flak and fighters.

German operational-level performance during the Velikiye Luki campaign was sub-par from beginning to end, largely due to underestimation of Soviet capabilities and terrain/weather factors. Von der Chevallerie had not developed a serious plan to conduct a relief operation, nor even bothered to ensure that the garrison had established procedures for aerial resupply. Once Velikiye Luki was surrounded, first von der Chevallerie then Wöhler allowed two understrength, non-mutually supporting relief operations to develop, which squandered valuable resources. Von Kluge and OKH also penny-pinched Gruppe Chevallerie, feeding individual battalions into battle rather than simply committing full divisions from the outset. Had von der Chevallerie been provided with two reinforced divisions from the beginning (which was just within the realm of German capabilities), it is likely that the relief operation could have reached Velikiye Luki and saved a substantial part of the garrison before it was overwhelmed. At the tactical level, the German troops in Velikiye Luki put up a superb defence against long odds and held off a far superior force for over six weeks. However, the loss of so many veteran junior leaders and NCOs was irreplaceable, and these kinds of defeats accelerated the tactical decline of the Wehrmacht.

The Soviet offensive to surround Velikiye Luki benefitted from surprise, thanks to excellent *maskirovka* and the massing of an overwhelming strike force on a narrow attack sector. In the opening moves, 3rd Shock Army was able to surround Velikiye Luki and nearly annihilated Gruppe Meyer, but thereafter Purkayev struggled to seize the victory that was within his grasp. Nevertheless, Soviet commanders remained ruthlessly focused on achieving their operational objectives, and ensured a steady supply of reinforcements to keep the pressure on the enemy. Reducing the Velikiye Luki garrison proved much tougher than anticipated, and 3rd Air Army's failure to interdict the Luftwaffe aerial resupply operation enabled the garrison to survive for several extra weeks. Consequently, 3rd Shock Army was forced to fight a protracted battle of attrition, which cost the Kalinin Front no fewer than 104,022 casualties in this sector, including 31,674 dead or missing. On the other hand, the soldiers of 3rd Shock Army, who suffered horrendous losses, should be credited with halting every single German relief effort through incredibly tough resistance. Although the campaign ended in a tactical victory, with the liberation of Velikiye Luki and the destruction of an important enemy garrison, 3rd Shock Army was too decimated to launch any further offensive operations. Victory without exploitation is a half-victory, which Stavka recognized.

By the scale of the Eastern Front in World War II, the six-week-long Battle of Velikiye Luki in 1942–43 seems to have been a relatively backwater action, involving just one Soviet army against a corps-size German force. Nevertheless, it was an important campaign that not only resulted in the death of over 40,000 of the combatants – far more than in most battles on the Western Front – but it seriously complicated the German situation in north–central Russia. Up until the defeats at Velikiye Luki and Stalingrad, Hitler's 'hold-fast' tactics had worked. Encircled garrisons at Demyansk and Kholm had survived for months, thanks to Luftwaffe aerial resupply and effective relief operations. Consequently, the annihilation of a well-prepared garrison in Velikiye Luki served to demonstrate the suicidal nature of 'hold-fast' tactics when circumstances were less than optimal. Once the Red Army demonstrated that it knew how to employ the firepower to overwhelm encircled garrisons, German generals became reluctant to rely upon 'hold-fast' tactics, and were more inclined to surrender territory before units were surrounded. Hitler recognized this ground shift in his generals' thinking, since it reflected a permanent shift of strategic initiative to the enemy.

THE BATTLEFIELD TODAY

Statue of Private Aleksandr Matrosov, 254th Rifle Regiment, who was killed in action near Velikiye Luki in late February 1943 and posthumously named a Hero of the Soviet Union. Matrosov actually died over a month after the liberation of Velikiye Luki in an obscure nearby village. The exact date of his death is ambiguous, but Soviet-era military historiography was more interested in highlighting sacrifice than worrying about details. (Author's collection)

After liberation, the city of Velikiye Luki was almost completely destroyed, with 91 per cent of its buildings burned down. Some effort was made to restore the city, but progress was slow, and given the devastation across western Russia took decades to complete. During the Soviet era, military historiography focused on the liberation of the region in 1943 and a handful of heroes, such as Private Aleksandr Matrosov. The main effort went into building the 'Obelisk of Glory', a 26m-high pillar topped with a star, in the Citadel; this project was completed in 1960. Interestingly, the Obelisk singles out the role of the 8th Estonian Rifle Corps in the liberation of the city, even though the Estonian performance in the campaign was marked by high levels of desertion. However, little else was done for decades to commemorate the battle, and foreign tourism in the region was negligible. The situation began to change in October 2008, when Russian President Dmitry Medvedev awarded Velikiye Luki the honourary title of 'City of Military Glory', for the courage demonstrated by its defenders in World War II. Following this recognition, Velikiye Luki began to encourage limited tourism and added a new historical museum and other public monuments. The 75th anniversary of the liberation in 2018 also saw an increase in commemorative efforts in the city.

Today, the best way to reach Velikiye Luki is to fly into St Petersburg and take the train to the city. There are some hotels and restaurants for foreigners, but like many Russian small cities, the number of attractions and services are limited. The only real relic of the 1942–43 siege is the fortress on the west bank of the Lovat, which has been partly reconstructed. Although some of the gates have been repaired, the one that Major Tribukait's troops used in January 1943 is still in poor condition. Outside the city, the areas where the heaviest fighting occurred are now unremarkable and bear few visible signs of historical significance, unless one is willing to go ploughing through marshland. Most of the villages that were fought over in 1942 and 1943

no longer exist. Using Google Earth imagery, German trenches are still clearly evident in several places, such as one area 5km west of Chernosem, deep in the forest. Most of hilltops in the area north-west of Chernosem likely still contain plenty of detritus of battle – including unexploded ordnance (mortar shells being one of the most typical hazards). As in most places in western Russia, here and there one may encounter small local markers alongside roads to commemorate partisans or aviators, but these are difficult to find without a guide.

Von Sass' bunker near the rail station still exists as a forlorn reminder of the battle. In the later stages of the battle, von Sass rarely left this shelter and surrendered here with his regimental staff. (Author's collection)

Aerial view of the reconstructed Velikiye Luki fortress in the 21st century, looking to the north-east. Note the T-34/85 tank memorial in the centre. The Lovat River is in the background, behind the line of trees. Note the railway bridge is just visible towards the upper right. (Author's collection)

FURTHER READING

Primary sources

Chronologische Übersicht des Oberkommandos der Heeresgruppe Mitte: *Der Kampf um Welikie Luki vom 24.11.1942–16.1.1943*, 1943

Erfahrungsbericht über die Kämpfe vor Walikije Luki, 26 January 1943, T-314, Roll 1512

Kriegstagebuch (KTB), 20.Infanterie-Division, 1942–43, NAM (National Archives Microfilm), Series T-315, Rolls 737

Kriegstagebuch (KTB), 83.Infanterie-Division, 1941–43, NAM (National Archives Microfilm), Series T-315, Rolls 1127-1129

Kriegstagebuch (KTB), 291.Infanterie-Division, 1942, NAM (National Archives Microfilm), Series T-315, Roll 1914

Kriegstagebuch (KTB), LIX.Armee-Korps, 1942–43, NAM (National Archives Microfilm), Series T-314, Rolls 1506–1512

Zhurnal Boyevykh deystviy, Kalininskogo Fronta 1942 [*Journal of Military Action, Kalinin Front, 1942*] on Pamyat-naroda.ru

Zhurnal Boyevykh deystviy, 184 tbr [*Journal of Military Action, 184th Tank Brigade, 20 March 1942–11 May 1943*] on Pamyat-naroda.ru

Secondary sources

Beloborodov, Afanasy P., *Vsegda v boyu* [*Always in Battle*], Moscow: Ekonomika, 1984

Carrell, Paul [Schmidt, Paul Karl], *Scorched Earth*, Atglen, PA: Schiffer Military History, 1994

Department of the Army Pamphlet No. 20-234, *Operations of Encircled Forces: German Experiences in Russia*, Washington, DC: Department of the Army, January 1952

Galitski, Kuzma N., *Gody surovykh ispytaniy, 1941–1944* [*Years of Harsh Testing, 1941–1944*], Moscow: Nauka, 1973

Haupt, Werner, *Die 8.Panzer-Division im 2. Weltkrieg*, Eggolsheim: Podzun-Pallas-Verlag, 1987

Isayev, Alexey V., *Kogda vnezapnosti uzhe ne bylo: Istoriya VOV, kotoruyu my ne znali* [*When the Surprise Was Gone: The History of the Second World War, Which We Never Knew*], Moscow: Eksmo, 2006

Kronik, Aleksandr L., *Boyakh za Velikiye Luki, Vospominaniya* [*Memories of the Battles for Velikiye Luki*], Voyenno-istoricheskiy zhurnal [*Military Historical Journal*], Moscow, No. 11, 1963

Kurowski, Franz, *Deadblock Before Moscow: Army Group Center 1942/1943*, West Chester, PA: Schiffer Publishing Ltd., 1992

Lyamin, Mikhail A., *Chetyre goda v shinelyakh* [*Four Years in Overcoats*], Izhevsk: Udmurtia, 1970

Muller, Klaus-Dieter (ed.), *Todesurteile Sowjetischer Militartribunale Gegen Deutsche (1944–1947): Eine Historisch-Biographische Studie* [*Death Sentences of Soviet Military Tribunals against Germans (1944–1947): A Historical-Biographical Study*], Göttingen: Vandenhoeck & Ruprecht, 2015

Schmidel, Toni, 'Welikije Luki, das Bollwerk im Sumpf' ['Velikije Luki, the Bulwark in the Swamp'], *Der Landser*, No. 654, 1970

Semyonov, Georgy G., *Nastupayet udarnaya* [*The Shock Comes*], Moscow: Military Publishing, 1986

Telek, Martin, *Der Fleischwolf von Rschew: Die Schlachten um Rschew und Welikije Luki 1942/43* [*The Meat Grinder of Rzhev: The Battles Around Rzhev and Velikiye Luki 1942/43*], Leipzig: Schelm, 2019

Tiemann, Reinhard, *Geschichte der 83.Infanterie-Division 1939–1945* [*History of the 83rd Infantry Division*], Bad Nauheim: Podzun, 1960

INDEX

References to images are shown in **bold**.